The Best Move:

Copyright © 2017 Lyudmil Tsvetkov

Contents

Introduction

This is a tactico-positional puzzle book. The intention will be to feature all the world champions, and we are starting with the greatest one, probably, Fischer.

Why not simply tactics book? Well, because tactics are just 50% of what chess is all about, and positional test suites are rather rare.

The book features 225 puzzles/positions, and is split in 2 parts, tactical and positional one. The tactical puzzles are 113, while the positional ones 112, so roughly equally split. I have been going through all of Fischer's games, equally checking for both types of puzzles, and in the end it proved the numbers are dead even.

Of course, it is a bit difficult to always categorise each position solution as either tactical or positional, as sometimes there is a mix of both, so I have simply chosen the dominating factor.

The more difficult of the positions have been checked with Stockfish not to commit any obvious mistakes. While doing this, I was surprised to learn Stockfish still does not see at least one third, but maybe even half, of the moves of the later Fischer in the positional set. That would point to the fact that the positional set is more difficult, as Stockfish has not a single problem with the tactical set.

Please note, that the aim is to just find the objectively best move, that will not always be a winning one. In this way, the riddles are closer in spirit to practical game situations, where there is not always mate in a specific number of moves, but maybe just a move that will give you some advantage. I guess there are an awful lot of books containing mate sequences.

The book features about one third of Fischer's games, seemingly he has left behind lots of masterpieces. If I had to define with a single word Fischer's puzzle collection, it would be elegance. So, apart from the usefulness of solving tests, the reader might also have the chance of enjoying quite some beauty.

The book does not have a key, as I found it to be easier for the reader when the puzzles and solutions share the same page, in that way one should not be constantly clicking here and there. You might simply want to try solving before looking at the solution, or even just read the explanations as comments to a specific position.

One of the upsides of this book is that it combines both tactical and positional puzzles, so you might learn both. Of course, if you prefer a particular set, you might concentrate just on it.

Fischer was, is and will remain a legend. Don't miss the chance to learn from the greatest!

December 2017

The tactical suite

1.

Black to move

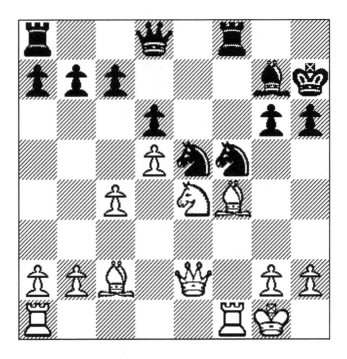

19...Nd4! Qd2 20...Nc4, winning a pawn, and then more material
21. Qf2 Rf4!, 21. Qd1 Nb2
(Thomason-Fischer, Lincoln 1955)

2.

Black to move

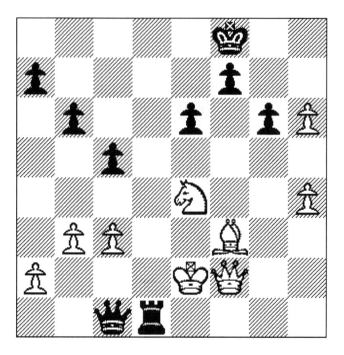

36...f5!, to kick the knight from e4, and then skewer the white king and queen with the rook on d2, winning the queen.
(Walz-Fischer, Montreal 1956)

3.

White to move

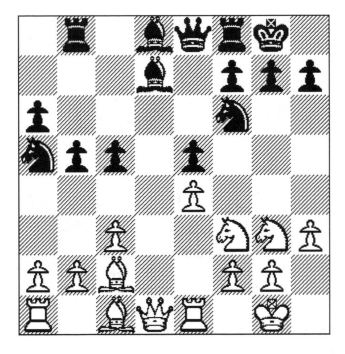

16. Qd6, attacking the rook on b8, as well as the pawns on c5, e5 and a6. The game continued 16...Nc6 17. Qc5 and Fischer won. (Fischer-Sharp, Montreal 1956)

White to move

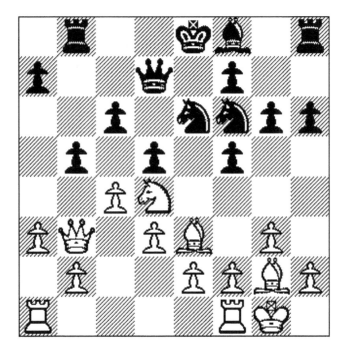

15. Nc6! Qc6 16. cd5 Nc5(the only way to save the knight) 17.
Qc3

17...Qd6(the queen should guard the knight on f6 that is also
attacked) 18. Bc5 Qc5 19. Qf6, 17...Qb6 18. b4 Na4 19. Qe5
check and then Bb6
(Fischer-Lapiken, Oklahoma 1956)

5.

Black to move

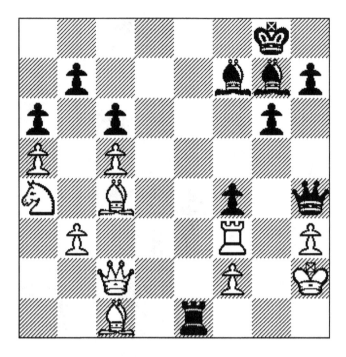

30...Qg5!(threatening mate on g1) 31. Bf7 Kh8(avoiding any queen checks) 32. Rg3 fg3 33. hg3 Rc1 and black wins.
(Donovan-Fischer, Oklahoma 1956)

6.

Black to move

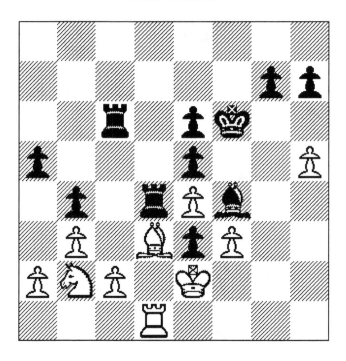

29...Rd3!
30. cd3 Rc2 and the knight falls, 30. Rd3 Rc2 similarly, 30. Kd3
Rc3 31. Ke2 Rc2, 30. Nd3 Rc2 31. Ke1 Bg3 32. Kf1 e2, forking
the king and rook
(Grossguth-Fischer, Philadelphia)

7

Black to move

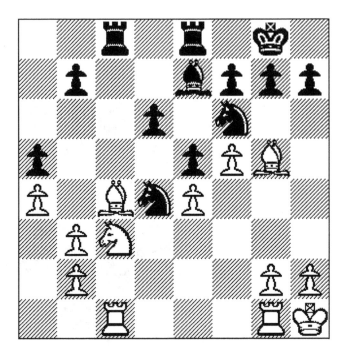

20...Ng4!, threatening smothered mate on f2 and the bishop on
g5, and black wins a piece.
(Blake-Fischer, Philadelphia 1956)

8.

White to move

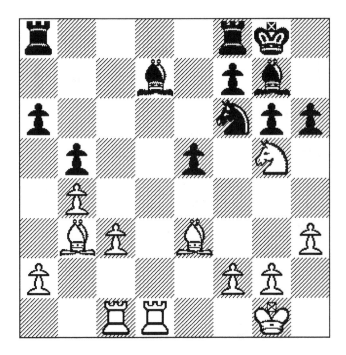

26. Ne4! Ne4 27. Rd7, winning the bishop pair. If the black light-square bishop retreats somewhere, then 27. Nf6 check Bf6 28. Bh6, picking up the h6 pawn.
(Fischer-Rinaldo, Cleveland 1957)

9.

White to move

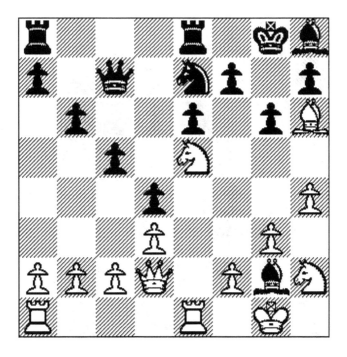

17. Nf7!, this saves the pawn and compromises the black pawn structure(e6 is now weak). Otherwise, after 17. Kg2 Be5, white is a pawn down.
(Fischer-Mednis, Cleveland 1957)

10.

White to move

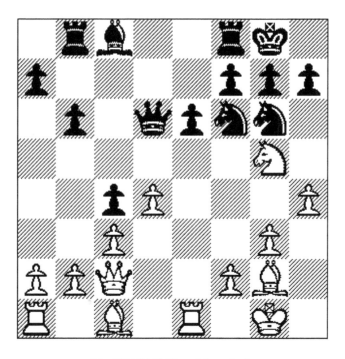

18. Nh7!!(I like this a lot).

If 18...Kh7, then 19. Bf4, skewering the queen and rook and winning the latter, as the knight on g6 is pinned to the white queen. After 18...Nh7 19. h5!, if the knight retreats, Bf4 will again reproduce the same skewer, while, if the knight does not retreat, hg6 simply wins a pawn. Very elegant solution on the part of Fischer.

(Fischer-Sherwin, East Orange, 1957)

White to move

21. c5!!(I give this two for elegance and surprise), the pawn threatens to advance to c6, so black should capture. Both captures lose, though. 21...Bc5 22. b4!, and the bishop can not move, because of the rook check on c8, picking the h8 rook. If 21...bc5, then 22. b4 again, and as the pawn similarly can not take due to the same combination, white will capture bc5 on the next move, creating a strong passed pawn, that will further go to c6. The black d4 pawn, on the other hand, is weak and should fall once the king gets to d3.

(Fischer-Sandrin, Milwaukee 1957)

Black to move

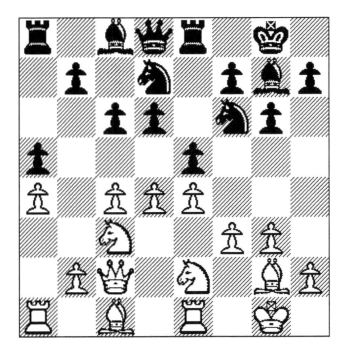

12...ed4! 13. Nd4 Qb6!, and white wins a pawn in all variations due to the very unpleasant absolute pin. 14. Nce2 Ne4 and then Bd4, 14. Rd1 Ne4 and Bd4, 14. Be3 Ng4!(here already 14...Ne4 might even lose due to 15. Ne6! and you will need an engine to see all complications) 15. hg4 Bd4, and later white will lose one of the g4 or c4 weak pawns.
(Surgies-Fischer, Milwaukee 1957)

13.

Black to move

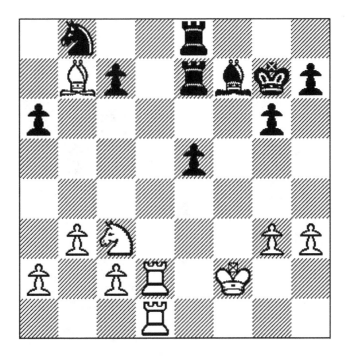

27...c6!, and the white bishop is trapped(28. Ba8 Ra7). That will win black 2 minor pieces for rook further on.
(Sobel-Fischer, New Jersey 1957)

White to move

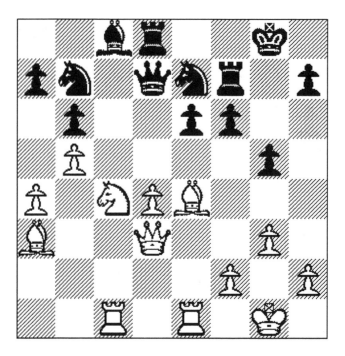

26. Bb7 Bb7 27. Nd6, and white wins the exchange. In case the rook on f7 moves, white gets even better with 28. Nb7 Qb7 29. Re6. Stockfish says Fischer's move was not best, though, pointing out 26. Red1 as significantly stronger. This kind of chess is not for humans, though.
(Fischer-Di Camillo, New Jersey 1957)

White to move

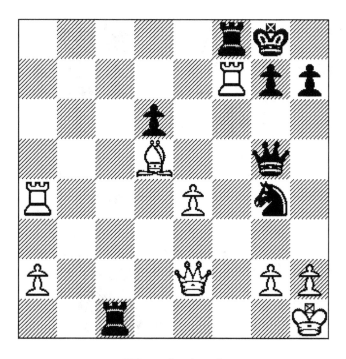

Who wins here?
Depends on what of the 2 realistically available moves white will choose. 31. Rf1? loses after 31...Kh8(now, the rook on f1 is attacked by both black rooks, Rf8 capture is impossible because the rook is pinned). 32. Rg1 Rg1 and Qc1, 32. Re1 Qh4 33. g3 Re1 34. Qe1 Rh2 mate, 32. Rd1 Rd1 33. Qd1 Nf2 and Nd1. If 32. Ra8, 32...Ra8 33. Ba8 Qf4 mates in around 10 moves. So, seemingly, white is losing. Fischer found the second option, though, **31. Qf1!!**(one of the most beautiful moves ever played), and now it is already white who is winning. The threat is Rf8 mate, so black has only option to take on f1. After 31...Rf1 32. Rf1 Qd5(32...Kh8 33. Rf8 mate) 33. Rf8 Kf8 34. ed5 white has enormous material advantage.
(Fischer-Sherwin, New York 1957)

16.

Black to move

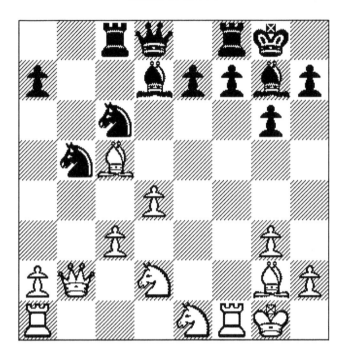

19...Nc3! 20. Qc3 Nd4!, and there are different lines, but black should win at least a minor piece in the end, it has simple too many threats: the bishop on c5 is attacked by the rook on c8, the white queen and rook on a1 by the bishop on g7, Ne2 fork check, etc. Severe development lag frequently leads to similar disastrous consequences. 20. Bc6 Ne2 check 21. Kf2 Rc6 22. Ke2 Rc5 is even worse.
(Kramer-Fischer, New York 1957)

Black to move

There are 2 realistic moves here: Rb1 and Rb4. One loses and the other wins. The trick is to find the right one. 49...Rb1? loses. 50. d7 Rd1(50...Re1 51. d8Q c1Q 52. Qf8 check Kh5 53. Bf3 mate) 51. d8Q Rd8 52. Rc1. Fischer played **49...Rb4!** check 50. Ka3(that is all the trick, the black king is now on a3, and the black pawn will promote on c1 with check) Rb1 and it is already black who wins.

(Lombardy-Fischer, New York 1957)

Black to move

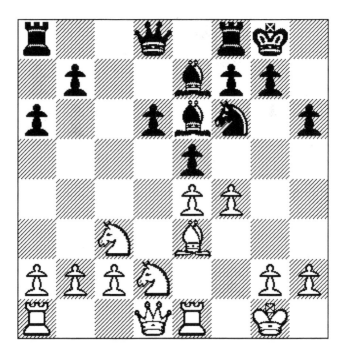

16...ef4! 17. Bf4 Qb6 check and then Qb2, picking up a pawn. 16...Ng4 is an alternative, but not that straightforward. (Bredoff-Fischer, San Francisco 1957)

White to move

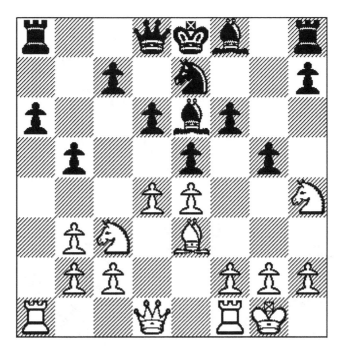

12. Qf3!!(the second exclamation mark is for the computer-style move in a pretty much unfamiliar setting), developing the queen. Now, if 12...Bg7, 13. Nf5 is very strong, as white enjoys significant lead in development. In the case of 12...gh4 13. Qf6 Qd7 14. d5!(but not 14. Qh8? Ng6 15. Qf6 Bg7, followed by ed4, and already black has the advantage) Bh3 15. gh3(but not 15. Qh8?? Qg4 16. g3 Qf3, mating) Qh3 16. Kh1 Bg7 17. Qg5 Qf3 check 18. Qg2 Qg2 19. Kg2, the ensuing endgame is winning for white.
(Fischer-Walker, San Francisco 1957)

White to move

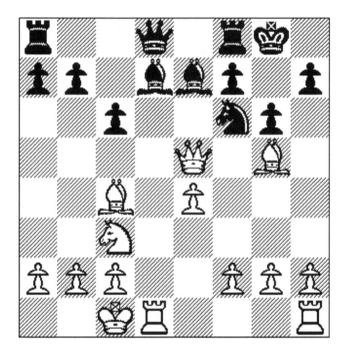

12. Rd7! Qd7 13. Bf6(13. Rd1 first might be even stronger),
winning 2 minor pieces for rook. If 12...Nd7, 13. Qe7 does the
same.
(Fischer-Goldsmith, West Orange, 1957)

21.

Black to move

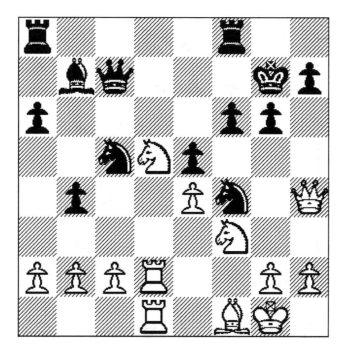

21...Bd5 22. cd5 Ne4, winning the exchange.
(Sanguinetti-Fischer, Bad Portoroz 1958)

White to move

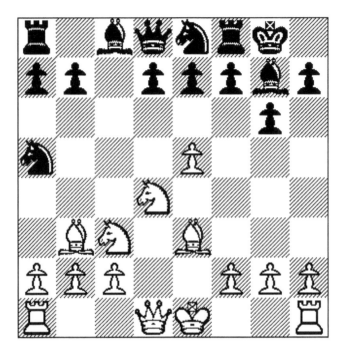

10. Bf7! Kf7(if 10...Rf7, 11. Ne6 wins the queen) **11. Ne6!!**(this is the culmination) de6 12. Qd8 and white wins. 11...Ke6 instead leads to quick mate after 12. Qd5 Kf5 13. g4 Kg4 14. Rg1 Kh4 15. Bg5 Kh5 16. Qd1. Very elegant again, as typical of Fischer.
(Fischer-Reshevsky, New York 1958)

Black to move

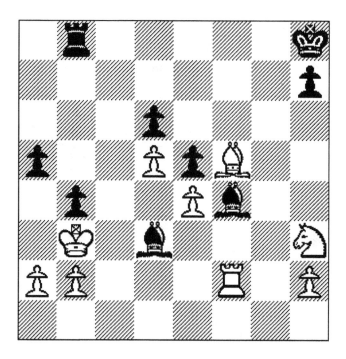

35...a4!(35...Be3 is equivalent) 36. Ka4 **b3!!**, another pawn sacrifice, that already is decisive, the white king will not be able to hide behind the b4 pawn any more, and the king is cut away along the b file to the edge of the board, so mating threats by the black rook and both black bishops become quite real. Now, if 37. ab3, then 37...Be3! 38. Bd7(38. Rf3 Ra8 check 39. Kb4 Bd2 mate) Bc5 39. Bc6(otherwise black mates on the a file) Rb6, and black mates or picks a lot of material. In the case of 37. a3, 37...Be3 38. Rg2 Bb5 39. Ka5 Bf1! decides.

(Souza Mendes-Fischer, Mar del Plata 1959)

White to move

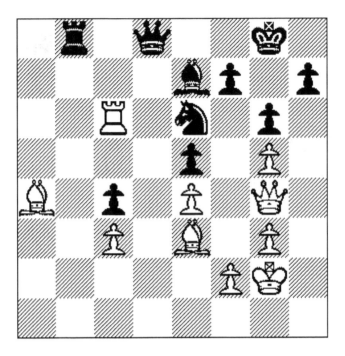

39. Re6! seals the game. Now, if 39...fe6 40. Qe6 Kf8 41. Qe5 is
more than convincing, while on the counter-trick 39...Qc8!,
pinning the rook to the undefended white queen, white has a
counter-counter-trick, **40. Bd7!!**(the 2 exclamations are for
elegance and because this is difficult to see by a human in the
search tree) Qd7 41. Rg6 check, winning the queen.
(Fischer-Shocron, Mar del Plata 1959)

Black to move

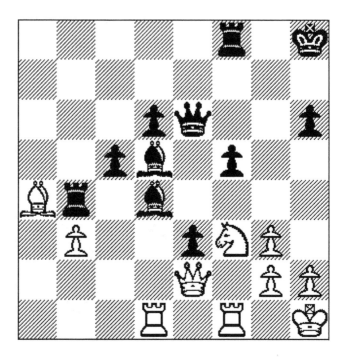

31...Ra4! 32. ba4 Bc4, followed by e2, forking both white rooks, and black wins a whole minor piece.
(Wexler-Fischer, Mar del Plata 1959)

Black to move

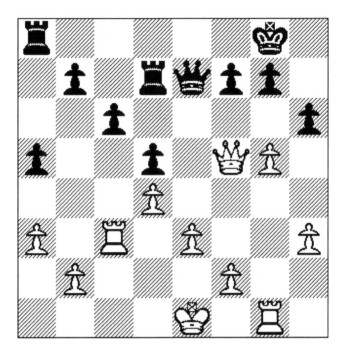

20...Rd6!, the only move that keeps the black advantage. 20...hg5 21. Rg5 and 20...h5 21. g6 both give white some edge, while on 20...g6, white has 21. gh6. Now, both 21. g6 hg6 22. Rg6 Rf8! and 21. h4 h5, and then g6, leaving the black king safe, with his counterpart just the opposite, are quite favourable for black. The only white chance seems to be 21. gh6.
(Denker-Fischer, New York 1959)

White to move

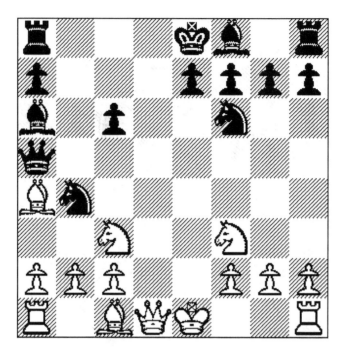

10. a3!, and the knight has no escape squares, as after 10...Nbd5
11. Bc6 and then Bd5, white similarly wins a piece. Curiously
enough, if white makes a random move, for example 10. h3, after
10...Rd8 11. Bd2 Ne4! 12. Ne4 Qa4, already black has the
advantage. So, it is very important in such double-edged positions
to find the right move.
(Fischer-Seidman, New York 1959)

Black to move

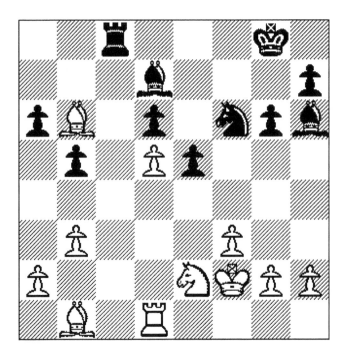

26...Bf5!, after light-square bishops are traded, the black rook will penetrate on c2.
(Romo-Fischer, Santiago 1959)

White to move

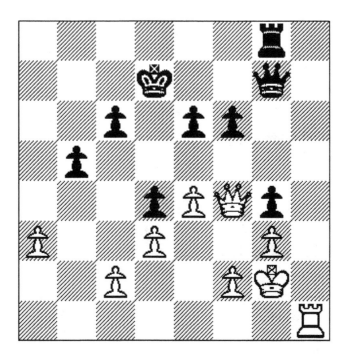

33. a4!, breaking open the game, to benefit from the exposed location of the black king. If 33...ba4, 34. Rb1 mates quickly, on 33...b4, 34. Rh5! Rc8(34...e5? 35. Qf5 and Rh7) 35. Ra5 swings the rook to the queen side with inevitable threats, while 33...Rh8 34. Rh8 Qh8 35. a5 creates a dangerous passer, which the black queen will take at some point, but in the meantime white will have picked up most of black's pawns.
(Fischer-Benko, Yugoslavia 1959)

White to move

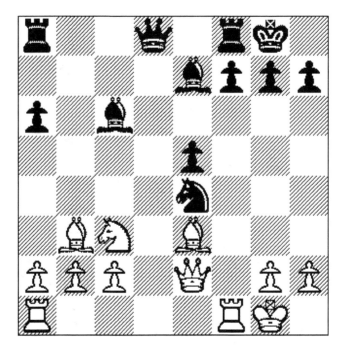

17. Rf7! Rf7 18. Bf7, winning a pawn and making the e5 pawn
isolated(18...Kf7 19. Qc4 check and Qc6).
(Fischer-Nievergelt, Zuerich 1959)

White to move

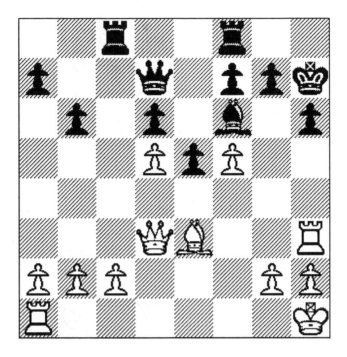

20. Bh6! gh6 21. Qd2 Bg7(21...Bg5 22. Qg5) 22. f6 Rh8(to protect the h6 pawn) 23. Qd3 check Kg8 24. fg7 Rh7 25. Rf1, and white should win at some point due to the weak black king shelter. Please note, that 20. Qd2 instead is a mistake, as the f5 pawn remains unprotected, and after 20...Qf5 21. Bh6 Kg8! black is already considerably better.
(Fischer-Kupper, Zuerich 1959)

32.

White to move

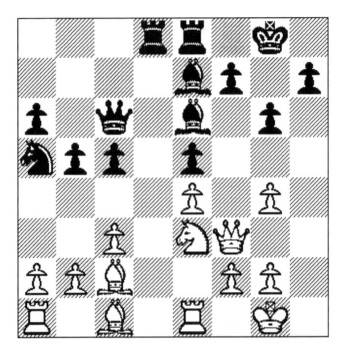

20. g5!, preparing the g4 square for the knight, using the fact that 20...Bg5 21. Nd5! Bd5 22. Bg5 Be6 23. Bd8 wins the exchange, while 21...Rd5 22. ed5 Bd5 23. Be4 Be4 24. Qe4 Qe4 25. Re4 Bc1 26. Rc1 leaves white the exchange for 2 pawns up, where the rook is stronger than a knight and 2 pawns into the late endgame. White is better also after 21...Bc1 22. Nf6 check Kh8 23. Rac1, as the dark squares of black are weak, but there is no complete certainty this is won.

(Fischer-Unzicker, Zuerich 1959)

White to move

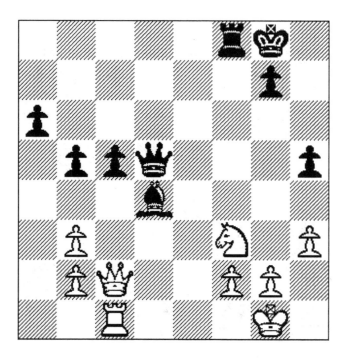

26. b4!, undermining the c5 pawn, after which the d4 bishop becomes weak. Now, both 26...c4 and 26...cb4 lose a piece to 27. Rd1 Rf4/Rd8 28. Qd2, and white threatens to capture bc5, creating a dangerous passed pawn. 26...Rc8 does not help, because of 27. Nd4 Qd4 28. bc5. The counter-sacrifice, 26...Rf3 27. gf3 Qf3 28. bc5 Qg3 29. Kf1 Qh3 30. Ke2 is also losing. Best chance for black was 26...Rf5!, but after 27. bc5 Bc5 28. Rd1 Qe6 29. h4!, making the black g pawn backward and preparing an excellent outpost square for the knight on g5, white should still be on top.

(Fischer-Bobotsov, Leipzig 1960)

34.

White to move

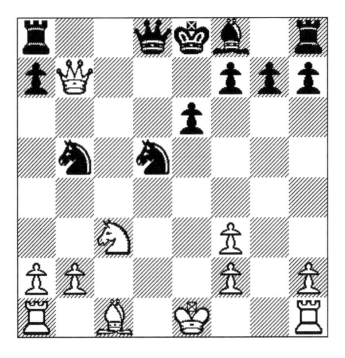

12. Qc6! check, as 12...Qd7 is impossible now, leaving the a8 rook unprotected, black must play 12...Ke7, losing castling rights with the black king exposed in the center, which after 13. Qb5 should give white some winning chances. 12. Qb5, the obvious capture, is much weaker, as 12...Qd7 simplifies the game into a dead drawn ending. Although the queen check most probably also only draws with perfect play, it is still the objectively and practically best option.

(Fischer-Euwe, Leipzig 1960)

Black to move

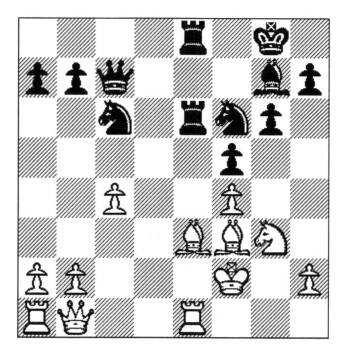

21...Re3! 22. Re3 Re3 23. Ke3 **Qf4!!**, great move, elegant and surprising. Now, 24. Kf4 Bh6! mates, similarly disastrous is 24. Kf2 Ng4 25. Kg2 Ne3 26. Kf2 Nd4
(Letelier-Fischer, Leipzig 1960)

Black to move

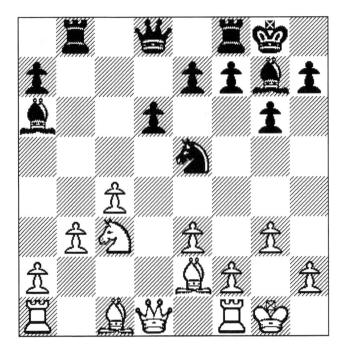

14...Nc4!, and after both 15. a4 Bc3 and 15. Qc2 Qa5 white is hopeless, losing a pawn or the exchange, while remaining much more passive at the same time.
(Saadi-Fischer, Mar del Plata 1960)

Black to move

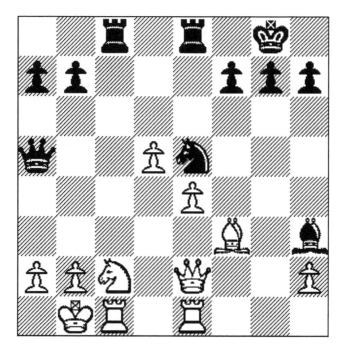

26...Rc2! is simple, but elegant tactics, winning the game. 27. Qc2 Nf3 28. Re3 Bg4 29. h3 Bh5 wins the exchange, 27. Kc2 Qa2 is even worse, while 27. Rc2 Nf3 28. Rec1(Qf3 capture is impossible, as the rook on e1 is hanging) Ne5 pretty much boils down to the same.

(Foguelman-Fischer, Mar del Plata 1960)

White to move

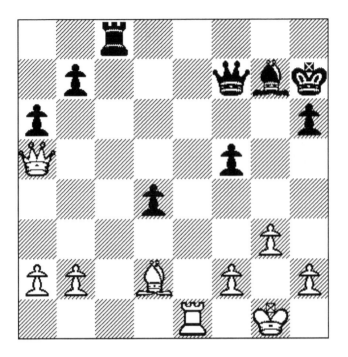

34. Re7! picks up the b7 pawn, as otherwise 34...Qe7 35. Qf5 loses the rook on c8 with check.
(Fischer-Olafsson, Mar del Plata 1960)

39.

Black to move

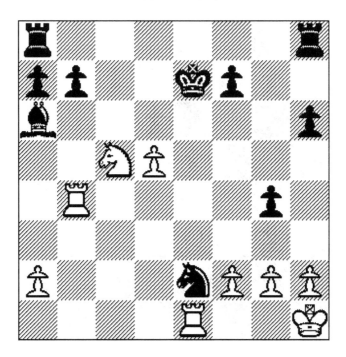

As if white will restore material equality after Na6 and Re2, but black has a subtle tactical resource that saves the piece and wins the game. **28...Rhe8!**(28...Rae8 and 28...Kd6 29. Na6 Rae8 are identical) 29. Na6 Kd6!, trapping the knight and threatening Ng3. 30. Rb2 fails to 30...Nd4 31. Re8 Re8 and the back rank is weak, white has no luft, so black will capture the knight on the next move.
(Bazan-Fischer, Mar del Plata 1960)

Black to move

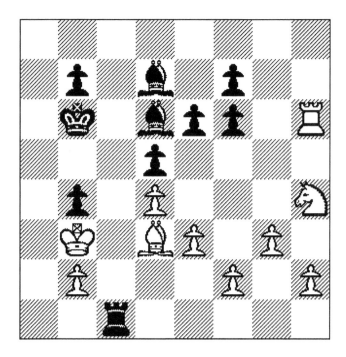

Even though material is equal, the white rook on h6 is badly off side, and this makes possible a decisive mating assault. **29...Ka5!**, with the king playing major role in it. Ba4, followed by b3 mate threatens, and white has a single move, 30. Ka2. 30...b3!, clearing the b4 square for the black king to advance even further, 31. Kb3 Ba4 check 32. Ka2 Kb4!(the king plays first violin here), threatening Bb3 mate again, 33. b3 Bb3 34. Kb2 Rd1, and black should mate shortly. Really and astounding and unusual king raid in the endgame.

(Letelier-Fischer, Mar del Plata 1960)

White to move

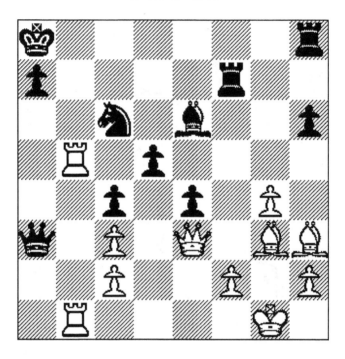

33. Qh6!, and white wins at least a piece, as 33...Rh6 34. Rb8
Nb8 35. Rb8 mate is impossible(33...Re8 34. Qe6). Please, note,
that a random move like 33. Kg2 could lead only to draw after
33...Qf8, while 33. Rc5 Rf3! even lose, so it is extremely
important to find such, sometimes not very obvious, tactics.
(Fischer-Weinstein, New York 1960)

42.

Black to move

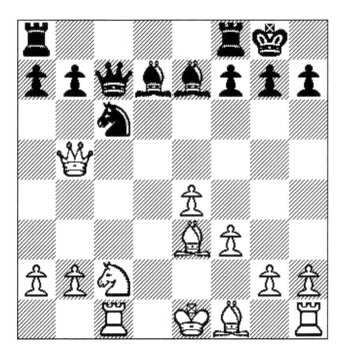

14...Nb4!, winning the exchange after 15. Nb4 Qc1 check 16. Bc1 Bb5 17. Bb5(17. Nd5 Bh4 18. g3 Bf1) Bb4. If 15. Qc4, then 15...Qa5!, threatening a discovered check 16. Nb4 Bb4 17. Kf2 Rac8. In the case of 15. Qe2, 15...Na2 16. Ra1 Rac8 should be sufficient for a win.

(Lombardy-Fischer, New York 1960)

Black to move

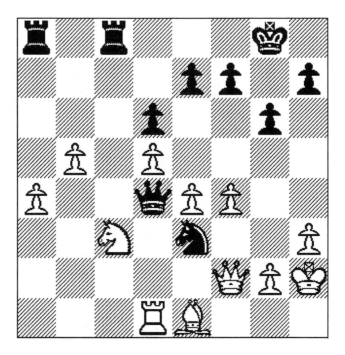

29...Qc3!, a bit paradoxical at first sight, but easily best. This leaves black after 30. Bc3 Nd1 and Nc3 with 2 rooks and a minor piece for queen and 2 pawns, more than sufficient compensation, and close to winning, in case white does not find the best moves. Other options are unsatisfactory. 29...Ne3?? 30. Qd4, 29...Qd1 30. Nd1 Nd1 31. Qd4 Rc1 32. a5! and the two connected pawns decide, 29...Qc5 30. Rb1 and white is better due to its connected passers.

(Bisguier-Fischer, New York 1960)

44.

Black to move

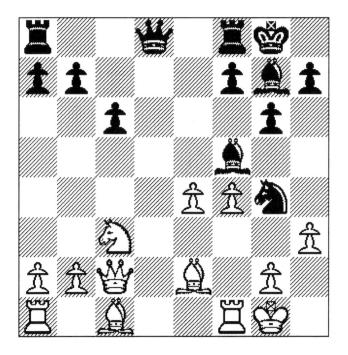

16...Qd4! check, leading to a long forced combination, which
after 17. Kh1 Nf2 18. Rf2(otherwise, black will capture on e4)
Qf2 19. ef5 Bc3!(removing the defender of the e2 bishop) 20. bc3
Rfe8 21. Bd3(all forced) Re1 check 22. Kh2 Qg1 23. Kg3 Rae8
leaves black much better due to the exposed location of the white
king and the pin on the a1 rook. White will have to find
extraordinary moves to attempt saving the game, something
difficult for a human in this position, as 24. Rb1 Rc1! 25. Rc1
Re3 26. Kh4 Qh2 should lose.
(Gudmundsson-Fischer, Reykjavik 1960)

45.

White to move

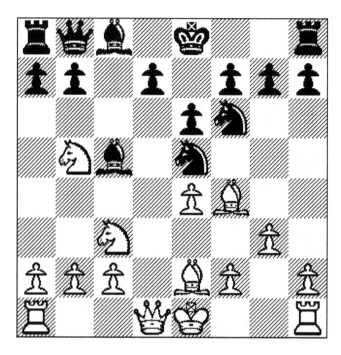

10. Be5!, using the fact black has not pushed d6, to gain couple of tempos after 10...Qe5 11. f4 Qb8 12. e5, simultaneously making the d7 shelter pawn backward. Now, 12...a6 13. ef6 ab5 14. fg7 Rg8 15. Ne4 Be7 16. Qd4 easily wins(14. Ne4 might be even better), while 12...Ng8 13. Ne4 and then Nd6 is even worse. Usually, trading bishop for knight would be counter-indicated, but specific position features fully justify that trade here. Specificities have a big role to play in chess.

(Fischer-Tal, Bled 1961)

White to move

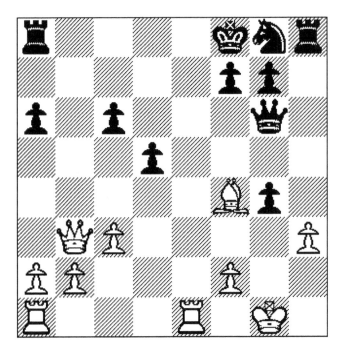

20. Qb7!, this wins rook in addition to the knight after 20...gh3 21. Bg3 Rd8 22. Qb4!(a retreat after an attack is always difficult to see) Ne7 23. Qe7 and Qd8, as the black rook has moved to a fork. 20. Qb4 instead wins only knight after 20...Ne7 21. Qe7 Kg8, and 20. hg4? Qg4 21. Bg3 Qh3 even loses. This comes to show how important it is to find the most accurate move in similar positions.
(Fischer-Geller, Bled 1961)

Black to move

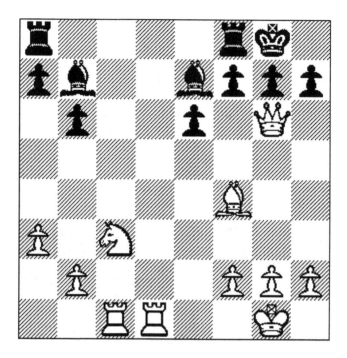

18...hg6?? loses a piece after 19. Rd7, forking both bishops. The right move is **18...fg6!**, attacking the bishop on f4 and gaining some tempos. In 95% of situations with similar setup the much better capture would be hg6 towards the center, so one should be very careful not to play automatically and mistake patterns for real game play.

(Bisguier-Fischer, Bled 1961)

Black to move

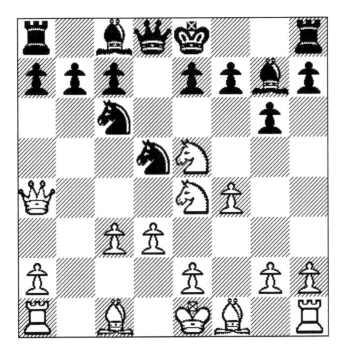

9...Nb6! wins a pawn after 10. Qb3 Ne5 11. fe5 Be5. 10. Qb5 instead, maintaining the pin, might be even worse after 10...a6 11. Qc5 Ne5 12. fe5 Nd7 and Ne5. It is frequently not very easy to see such winning retreats, as that involves surprise.
(Larsen-Fischer, Copenhagen 1962)

White to move

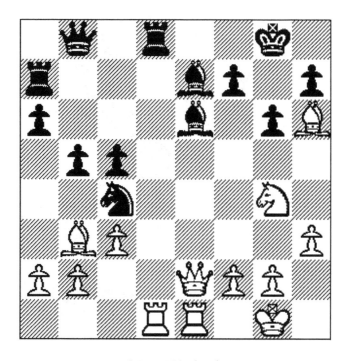

25. Rd8! check
Now, if 25...Bd8 26. Bc4! bc4(otherwise, white mates on e8) 27.
Qc4!, winning. If 25...Qd8 instead, again 26. Bc4 seals it; 26...bc4
27. Qe5, or 26...Bc4 27. Nf6 Kh8 28. Qe5.
(Fischer-Keres, Curacao 1962)

50.

Black to move

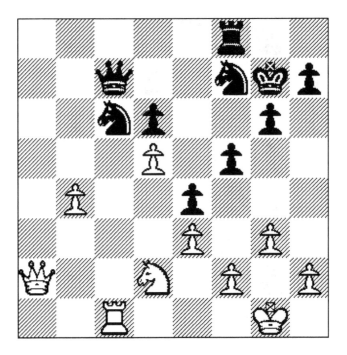

32...Qa7!, winning a piece after 33. Qa7 Na7, as the queen on a2 is unprotected. 33. Qb2 check is met by Nce5.
(Kortchnoi-Fischer, Curacao 1962)

White to move

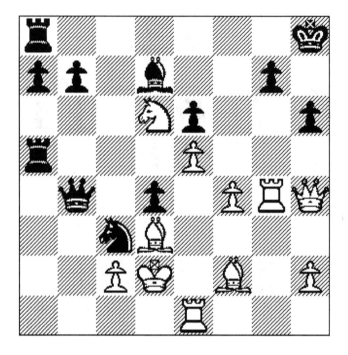

31. Qh6!
31...gh6 32. Nf7 mate, 31...Kg8 32. Qg7 mate
(Fischer-Benko, Curacao 1962)

White to move

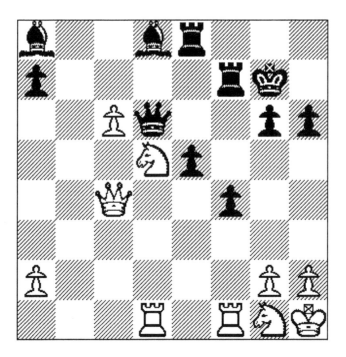

31. Nf4!, opening the f line, so that the queen and the rook on f1 target the black f7 rook simultaneously, giving rise to different tactics. Each reply loses easily. 31...Qc6 32. Nh5 check Kh8(otherwise white checks on f7 with the queen) 33. Qc6 Bc6 34. Rf7, 31...Qe7 32. Rd7, 31...Qc7 32. Ne6 Re6 33. Qe6, 31...Qf8 32. Rd8!, deflecting the rook from guarding the e6 square, ef4 33. Qd4 check and Rd6.

(Fischer-Berliner, New York 1962)

White to move

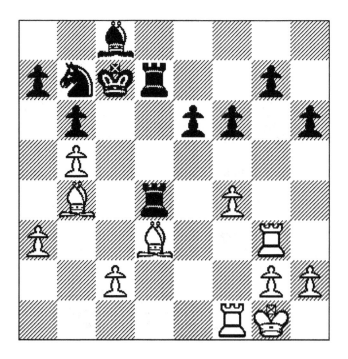

26. Bf8!, taking aim at the g7 and h6 pawns, after which white easily wins. Although after Bf8 is played, the weakness of the black pawns and their capture are obvious, making the move itself is a bit tricky, as this is an unusual manoeuver. Miss white that move or 26. f5, which also wins, though slower, and the game gets close to equal after Nb7-c5.
(Fischer-Addison, New York 1962)

White to move

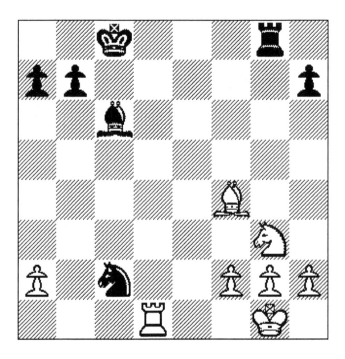

26. Nf5!, with a mate threat on e7 and a simultaneous fork. The black king can not move, and the rook has just 2 available squares, preventing mate. 26...Re8 27. Nd6 loses the exchange, while 26...Rg2 check 27. Kf1 b6(only move, as Ne7 mate still threatens) 28. Ne7 Kb7 29. Nc6 Rg4 30. Nd8 check and Ne6 a piece.
(Fischer-Sherwin, New York 1962)

White to move

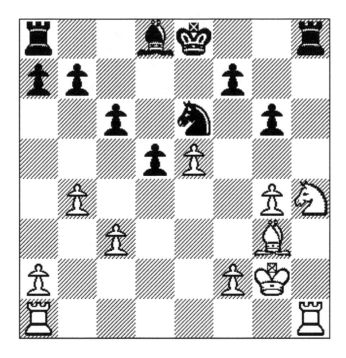

24. Nf5!, and now gf5 is impossible because of Rh8. After 24...Rh1 25. Nd6 check Kf8 26. Rh1, white has posted an excellent knight on d6 and gained control of the h file in a single manoeuver. The possible continuation, probably optimal for black, 26...a5 27. b5(no opening of the a file allowed), followed by f4-f5, leaves white close to winning.
(Fischer-Bisguier, New York 1962)

White to move

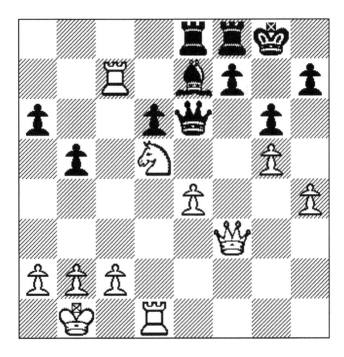

29. Nf4! Qe5 30. Rd5, sending the queen off-side to h8 or g7. Black is so cramped for space, the black pawns on the queen side weak and h4-h5 threatens in a range of lines, so there is little doubt as to the outcome of the game. f7-f6 freeing attempt fails to Ne6 fork with the queen on g7 and Qb3 x-ray attack upon the king with the queen on h8. If white makes a waiting move, however, like 29. a3, for example, then 29...f6 is already a possibility, and black gets rid of big portion of the cramp, with much more acceptable position, although still lost.
(Fischer-Bolbochan, Stockholm 1962)

Black to move

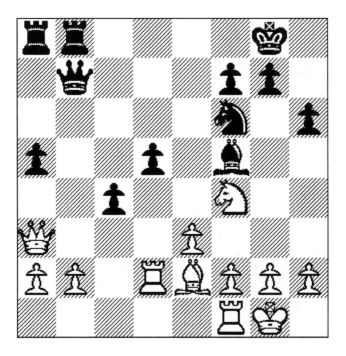

21...g5! is already too much for white. 22. Nd5 Nd5 23. Bf3 Bd3!
wins black a piece, while 22. Nh5 Ne4 or 22. Nh3 Ne4 further
increase the black initiative. White has to find the computer-like
22. g4! to have minimal survival chances. Playing 21...Ne4
straight is impossible because of 22. Rd5
(Bertok-Fischer, Stockholm 1962)

White to move

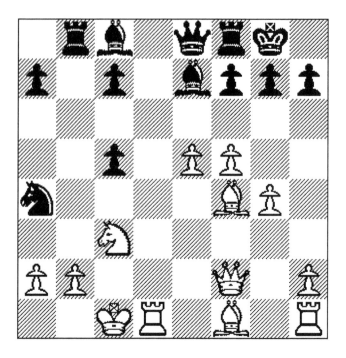

Black threatens to capture on b2, and 21. Na4 Qa4 is too
dangerous. White has however a smart tactical option at his
disposal, **21. Bb5!**, and after the forced 21...Rb5 22. Na4 Rb4 23.
Nc3 the white king is safe, while white retains all his relative
positional advantages.
(Fischer-German, Stockholm 1962)

White to move

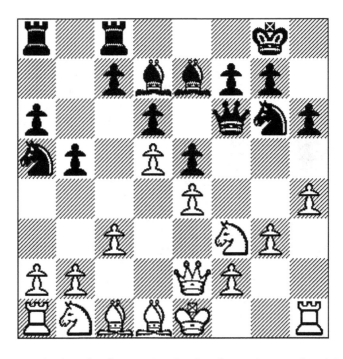

15. Bg5!, nicely winning queen for 2 minor pieces after 15...hg5
16. hg5 Qg5 17. Bg5 Bg5. Such moves should not be missed, as
otherwise, black is fine after 15. h5 Nf8, or 15. Na3 Bd8,
preparing an escape square for the queen on e7. 15. b4 Bd8 16.
ba5 c6 is also winning, but less convincingly so.
(Fischer-Ciocaltea, Varna 1962)

Black to move

14...Qc6!, threatening mate on g2, followed by Qb5, wins one of
the bishops on the b file. It might be simple, but is still elegant
and very efficient.
(Rivera-Fischer, Varna 1962)

Black to move

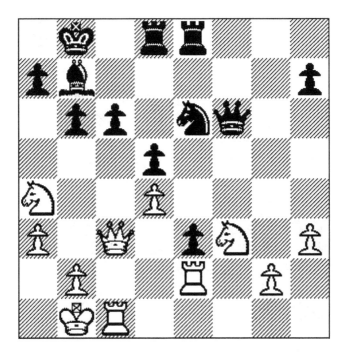

28...c5!, supporting and challenging the d4 square at the same time. 29. dc5 d4 and 29. Rd1 cd4 both leave black with 2 connected central e and d passers, 29. Re3 cd4 wins the exchange, while 29. Qe3 Nd4! 30. Qe8 Re8 31. Re8 Kc7 is also easily winning(Qg6 fork threatens). 28...Nf4 29. Re3 Ne2, forking queen and rook also wins.

(Silwa-Fischer, Warszawa 1962)

62.

White to move

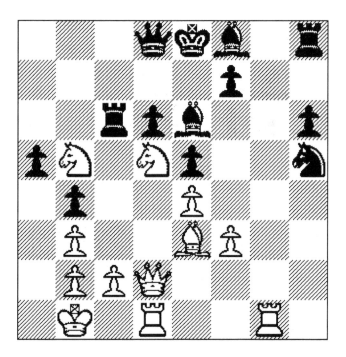

23. Na7!, other moves also win, but that is the most obvious and straightforward one. 23...Ra6 24. Qe2 Ra7 25. Ba7(24...Bc8? 25. Nc8 Qc8 26. Qa6! Qa6 27. Nc7), 23...Bd5 24. Qd5(24...Ra6? 25. Qb5 forking check, 24...Rc7 25. Bb6 pin).

(Fischer-Leopoldi, Bay City 1963)

White to move

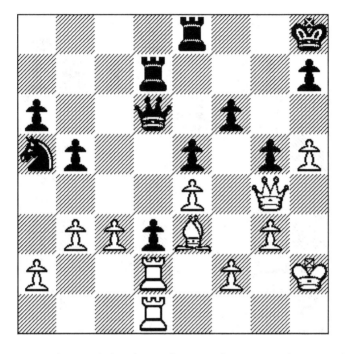

34. Rd3! Qd3 35. Qd7, the endgame after 35...Qd7 36. Rd7 is
fully hopeless.
(Fischer-Bisguier, New York 1963)

White to move

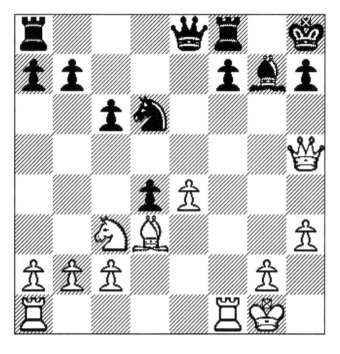

The white queen and the bishop on d3 attack the h7 square, one directly, the other on an x-ray. How to use that fact? 19. e5? fails to 19...f5(attacking the queen) 20. Qe8 Ne8 21. Na4 Be5 22. Nc5 Nd6, drawing. **19. Rf6!!**, great move. The rook immobilises the f7 pawn, and now e4-e5 tremendously gains in force. 19...Bf6 20. e5 Nf5 21. Bf5, with mate on h7 to follow. 19...h6 20. e5(threatening Rh6 check and Rh8) Kg8 21. Ne4, similarly. 19...dc3 20. e5 is identical, of course. Astounding elegance!
(Fischer-Benko, New York 1963)

65.

Black to move

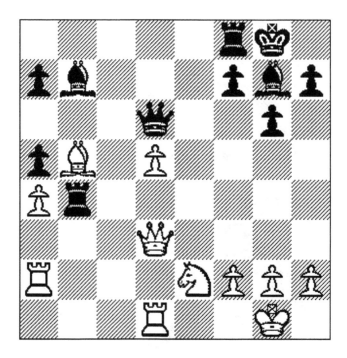

23...Qd5! 24. Qd5 Bd5, and black wins. 25. Rd5 Rb1 check 26. Nc1 Rc1 27. Bf1 Rb8 28. f4 R8b1 29. Rf2 Bf8, followed by Bc5. 25. Rad2 Bb3 26. Rc1 a6, with more than sufficient material and positional advantage.

(Greenwald-Fischer, Poughskeepsie 1963)

Black to move

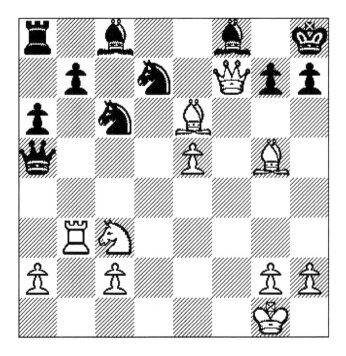

It seems as though black should lose, as it can not defend simultaneously the g8 square and the bishop on f8, 19...Nf6 20. Qf8 with mate, but black has a resourceful defence. **19...Qc5!** check, defending the f8 bishop, 20. Kh1 **Nf6!!**(the second exclam is for elegance again), protecting the g8 square, while Be6 threatens, 21. ef6 Be6 22. Qe6 Qg5, and black retains the piece more with all mate threats having evaporated. 20. Be3 Qe3 21. Kf1 Qc1 check 22. Kf2(22. Ke2 Nd4 and Ne6) Bc5 does not save white at all.

(Tringov-Fischer, Havana 1965)

Black to move

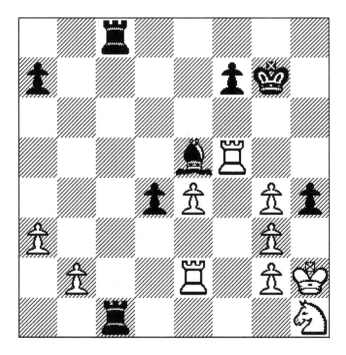

41...Rh1! Other moves also win, but this one forces mate after 42.
Kh1 Rc1 42. Kh2 hg3 and Rh1.
(Bisguier-Fischer, New York 1965)

Black to move

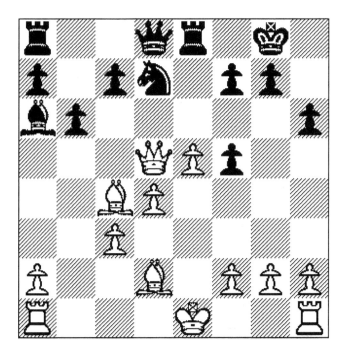

15...Ne5! The knight defends the vulnerable f7 point. 16. Qd8 Nc4 check 17. Qe8 Re8 18. Kd1(18. Be3 f4) Nd2 19. Kd2 Re2 and Rf2 wins easily. 16. de5 Qd5 17. Bd5 Re5 and Rd5 is also hopeless. The alternative, 15...Bc4 16. Qc4 is very close to a draw.

(Saidy-Fischer, New York 1965)

White to move

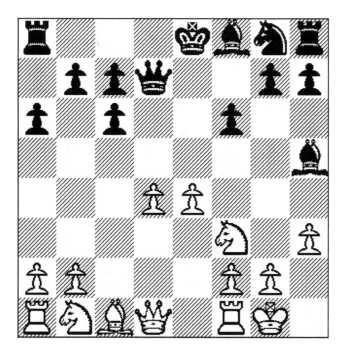

10. Ne5! This will win back black's pair of bishops in all lines.
10...Bd1 11. Nd7 Be2 12. Re1 Kd7 13. Re2, retaining much better
pawn structure, especially in the center, 10...Qh3 11. gh3 Bd1 12.
Rd1 fe5 13. fe5, similarly. 10...Bd1 11. Nd7 Bc2 12. Nf8 and then
Nc3 might be even worse. Interestingly, Stockfish does not quite
see that move.
(Fischer-Jimenez, Havana 1966)

70.

White to move

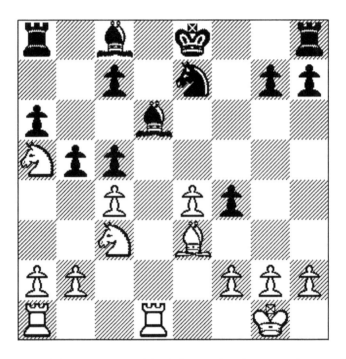

If the white bishop retreats, black has gained tempo, increasing its drawing chances. **14. e5!**, this subtle tactical trick allows white to fight for the initiative. 14...Be5 15. Bc5 is bad for black, as its king is exposed to attacks. After 14...fe3 15. ed6 ef2 check 16. Kf2 0-0 17. Kg1 cd6 18. Rd6 white retains a visible edge.
(Fischer-Portisch, Havana 1966)

71.

Black to move

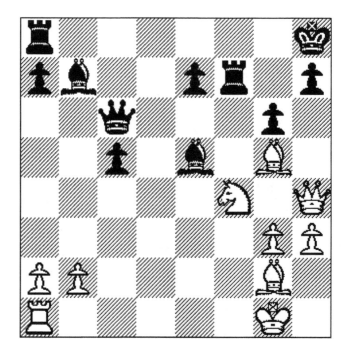

26...Rf4!

26...Bd4 check transposes. Other moves, like 26...Qb6, also win, but this is the most effective one. After 27. Bc6(otherwise black mates on g2) Bd4 28. Kh2 Rf2 the black attack, combining couple of heavy pieces and couple of bishops, is so heavy, that white gets mated soon or loses too much material.

(Johannessen-Fischer, Havana 1966)

White to move

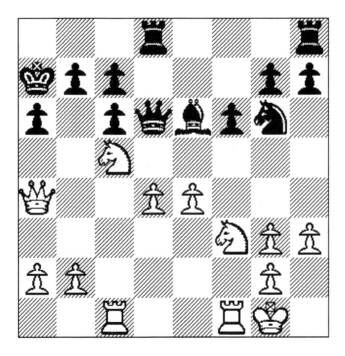

18. Na6! It is as if I am watching Stockfish outplay Komodo in this Ruy Lopez line on my computer. 18...ba6 19. Rc6 loses at least the queen. 18...Qg3 19. Rc6! and 18...Bh3 19. e5 are not a tiny bit better.

(Fischer-Gligoric, Havana 1966)

Black to move

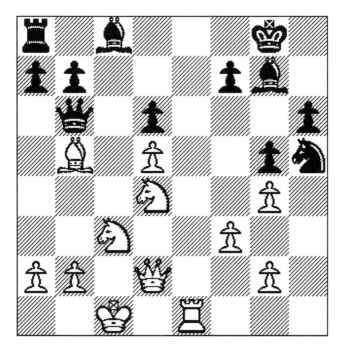

21...Bg4!, winning a pawn after 22. Ne2 Bc8 23. g4 a6! 24. Ba4 Nf6. 22. fg4 Bd4 23. gh5 Bc3 and Qb5 is even worse. 21...Bd4 instead should lead only to a draw. If black plays 21...Nf6, then after 22. Kb1 a6 23. Ba4 white is slightly better, and 21...Nf4? 22. Re8 check, unpleasantly pinning the c8 bishop, Kh7(22...Bf8 should not change anything) 23. Ne6!! fe6 24. Qf4!, threatening Bd3 mate, even loses. Fischer indeed played like a computer in his later career.

(Yepez-Fischer, Havana 1966)

White to move

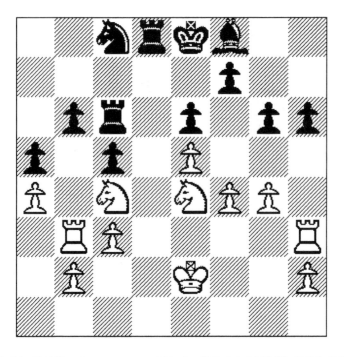

33. Na5! Winning a pawn. 33...ba5?? 34. Nf6 Ke7 35. Rb7
(Fischer-Durao, Havana 1966)

White to move

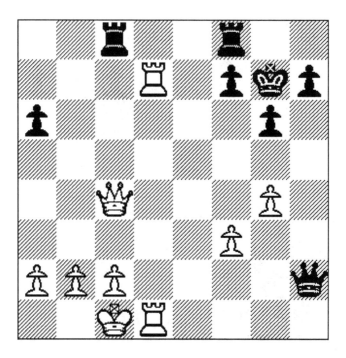

24. Rf7! check, this is the simpler, stronger and much more elegant solution than 24. Qd4. After 24...Rf7(24...Kh6 25. g5! leaves the black king into the open, with little chances of survival) 25. Qc8 Qf4 check 26. Kb1 Qf3 27. Rc1, white is largely winning.

(Fischer-Reshevsky, New York 1966)

White to move

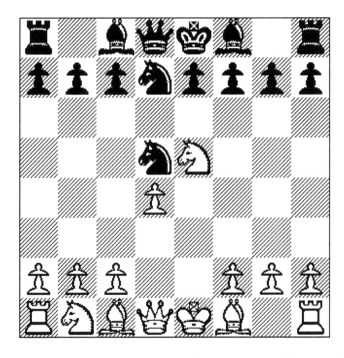

Larsen largely misplayed the opening. **6. Nf7!**, after 6...Kf7 7. Qh5 check Ke6 8. c4! N7f6 9. cd5 white is much better and most probably winning.
(Fischer-Larsen, Santa Monica 1966)

White to move

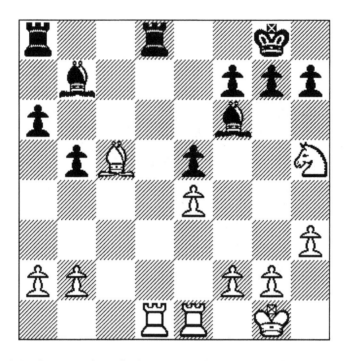

26. Nf6! gf6 27. Rd8 Rd8 28. Be7 Rd4 29. Re3!(threatening Rg3 check and Bf6 mate), and then white will capture on f6 and, although black might take on e4, the e5 weak pawn will soon fall, leaving white with a pawn more and much superior pawn structure, which, even with opposite colour bishops present, might give good winning chances.
(Fischer-Forintos, Monaco 1967)

Black to move

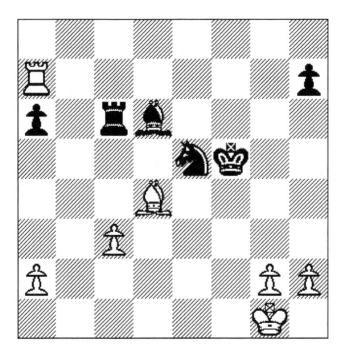

27...Rc3!, winning a pawn more. 28. Bc3 Bc5 check and Ba7, 28.
Ra6 Rc1 29. Kf2 Ng4 and then picking the h2 pawn.
(Mazzoni-Fischer, Monaco 1967)

White to move

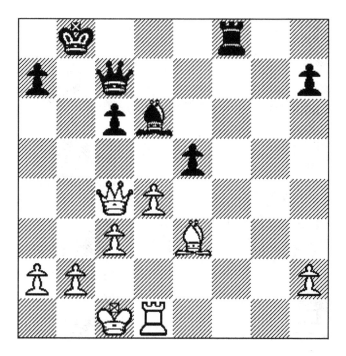

29. de5!, winning a further pawn. 29...Be5?? 30. Qb4, forking
king and rook.
(Fischer-Bergraser, Monaco 1967)

White to move

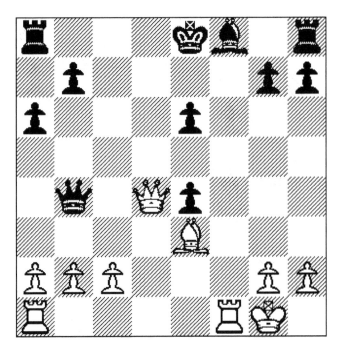

16. Rf8! check, very elegant, though more or less obvious.
16...Rf8/Kf8 17. Qb4, 16...Qf8 17. Qa4, winning. If 17...b5, then
18. Qe4 Rd8(nothing better) 19. Qc6 Rd7(19...Ke7 20. Bc5,
19...Kf7 20. Rf1) 20. Rd1 Qe7 21. Bb6, with Qc8 to follow. In the
case of 17...Kd8, 18. Bb6 Kc8 19. Qc4 Kd7 20. Qc7 Ke8 21. Qb7
seals it.
(Fischer-Dely, Skopje 1967)

White to move

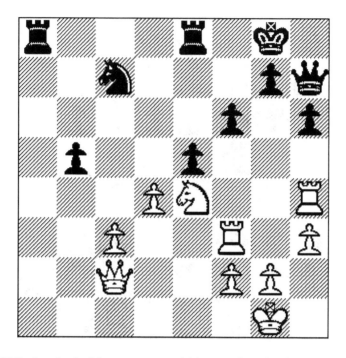

28. Nf6! check, forking queen and king. After the forced 28...gf6
29. Rg3! Kh8(otherwise, the black queen falls) 30. Qc1(targeting
the h6 square and threatening Rh6) h5 31. Qd1 the black queen
falls, as Rh5 is inevitable.
(Fischer-Panov, Skopje 1967)

White to move

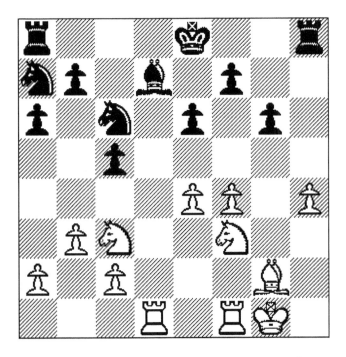

26. Na4!, that wins the c5 pawn. Frequently, people are even unwilling to consider knight moves on the edge.
(Fischer-Bukic, Skopje 1967)

White to move

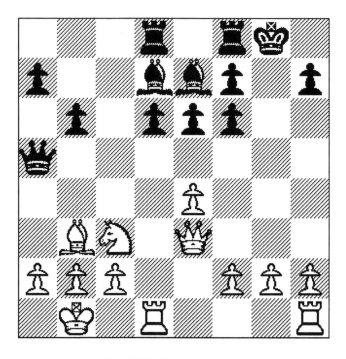

15. Nd5!!(for elegance)

After 15...ed5 16. Rd5 Qa6(16...Qb4 17. c3) 17. Rh5, followed by
Qh6, white mates(17...Bg4 18. Qg3). Please note, though, that
playing 17. Qh6? instead of Rh5 lets black slip 17...Bc6! 18. Rh5
Be4, and the bishop defends the h7 square. So, one must be very
careful in such highly tactical situations. The alternative,
15...Rfe8 16. Ne7 Re7 17. Rd6 wins white a pawn, but the pin on
the d file should bring more material later.
(Fischer-Sofrevski, Skopje 1967)

White to move

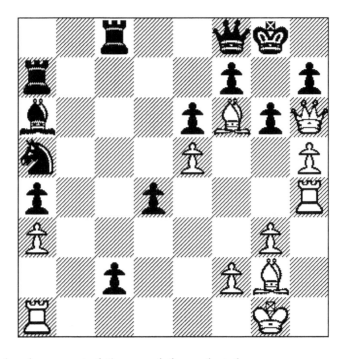

This has been posted thousand times, but deserves one more. **31. Qh7!!** mates in 3 moves. 31...Kh7 32. hg6 double check Kg6(32...Kg8 33. Rh8 mate) 33. Be4 mate. Elegance at its best. (Fischer-Miagmasuren, Sousse 1967)

White to move

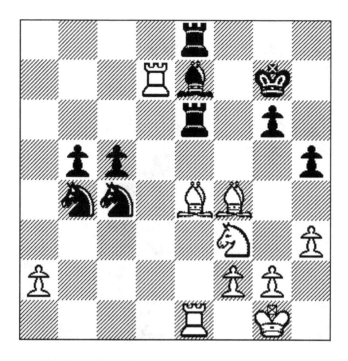

34. Ng5 Rf6 35. Bf3! Rf4 36. Ne6 wins the exchange. 35...Kf8
36. Nh7 and Nf6 is even worse.
(Fischer-Stein, Sousse 1967)

White to move

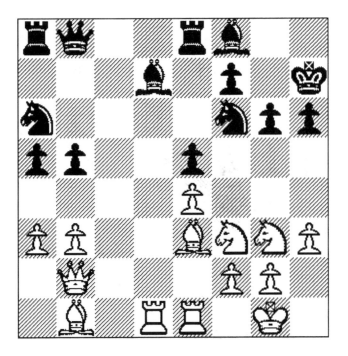

26. Ne5!, simple, but very effective. 26...Qe5 27. Bd4 Qc7 28. Bf6 gives white thrashing advantage. 26...Re5 27. Bf4 Bd6 28. Rd6! Qd6 29. Be5 and Bf6 loses even more material. 26...Be6 27. Nf7 is equally hopeless.

(Fischer-Reshevsky, Sousse 1967)

White to move

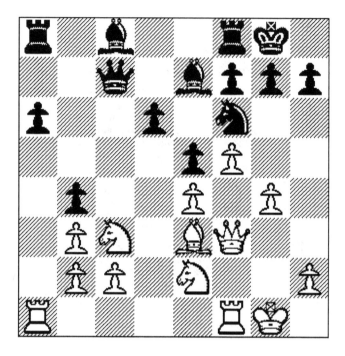

16. g5!, instead of retreating its knight, white should attack the enemy knight, of course. After 16...bc3(16...Ne8 or 16...Nd7 is too passive and loses quickly after 17. Nd5) 17. gf6 Bf6 and a recapture on c3, white is considerably better.

(Fischer-Hamann, Nathania 1968)

White to move

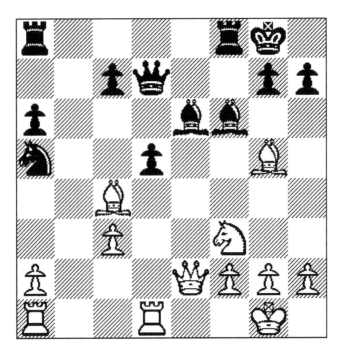

17. Qe6! check, this is as simple as elegant, so I want to feature it. After 17...Qe6 18. Bd5 Qd5 19. Rd5 Bc3 20. Rc1 c6(20...Bb4 21. Rc7 is even worse) 21. Rd3(Rd7 is an alternative) white gets quite some edge, the c pawn should fall at some point, with nice chances to convert.
(Fischer-Ree, Nathania 1968)

Black to move

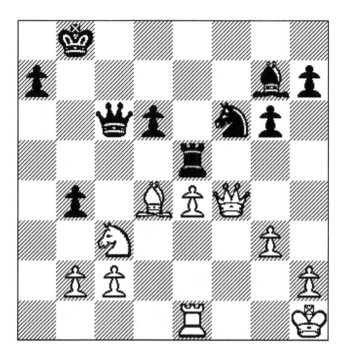

25...Rf5!, the e4 white pawn is pinned and can not capture, and after the white queen retreats, black takes on c3, staying with a piece more. 25...Re6 26. Ne2 Re4 27. Qf3 might also win, but is far less effective. Taking on c3, 25...bc3 26. Be5 de5 27. Qe5 is very close to a draw. It is not every day that a rook attacked by a minor piece goes to a square, attacked by an enemy pawn. That is why the move is psychologically difficult to see.
(Bernstein-Fischer, Nathania 1968)

White to move

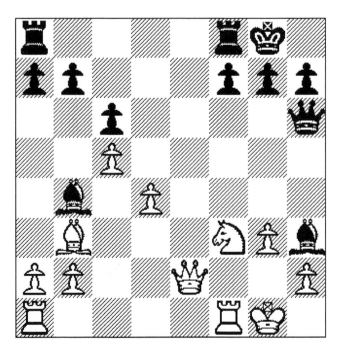

20. Ne5!, immediate counter-attack on the f7 square, regardless of the material lost. This should decide, either promptly or later into the endgame, as 20...Be6 is impossible because of 21. Nf7!, attacking the queen, 21...Bf7(21...Rf7 22. Qe6) 22. Rf7 Rf7 23. Rf1. The alternative, 20. Rf2? loses a tempo and should draw after 20...Rae8 21. Ne8 Be6, as this time the bishop on e6 is safely guarded.
(Fischer-Minic, Vinkovci 1968)

91.

Black to move

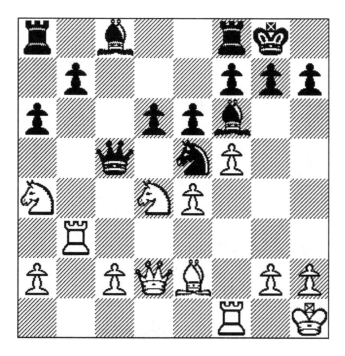

Now, if the queen retreats, white pretty much equalises the game after 16...Qc7 17. Nb6 Rb8 18. a4! and a5. But black has much better. **16...Nc4!**, excellent counter-attack that wins a piece due to particular piece dislocations. 17. Bc4 Qc4, simultaneously attacking the rook on f1 and both knights on d4 and a4, 17. Qb4/Qc3 Qd4 18. Qc4 Qc4 19. Bc4 b5!, forking both minor pieces.

(Matov-Fischer, Vinkovci 1968)

Black to move

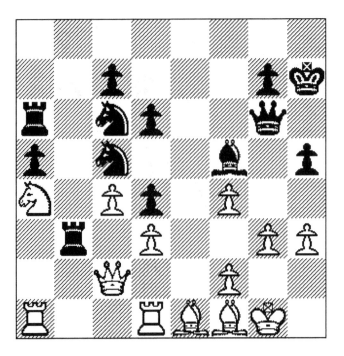

26...Rd3!!, this is a bit difficult to see tactically, hence the 2 exclams. 27. Nc5 Rd1 28. Qd1 bc5 should win for black. In above line, 27...Rg3 check instead is a mistake, as after 28. fg3 Bc2 29. Na6 Bd1 30. Rd1 white has nothing to fear because of the majority of its pieces. 27. Bd3/Rd3 Nd3 is even worse. Please note, that 26...Bd3? is a huge blunder, although very difficult to see by a human over the board, as after 27. Rd3! Rd3 28. Nc5 Rg3 check 29. fg3 Qc2 30. Bd3 check suddenly forks the black queen and king, winning. So, Fischer actually calculated like a machine.

(Saidy-Fischer, New York 1969)

White to move

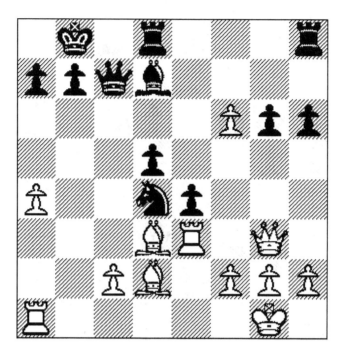

23. Re4!!, extreme elegance, although easy to see. This wins a
pawn. Capturing the rook is impossible, because Bf4 pins the
queen. After 23...Qg3 24. Rd4 the queen is attacked by two white
pawns and should retreat. If it does so on the h2-b8 diagonal, then
Bf4 regains it due to the existing pin. 23...Qg4 24. Rg4 Bg4 25.
Bg6 is even worse, as white gets the bishop pair, two pawns and
dangerous passers for the exchange.
(Fischer-Schweber, Buenos Aires 1970)

White to move

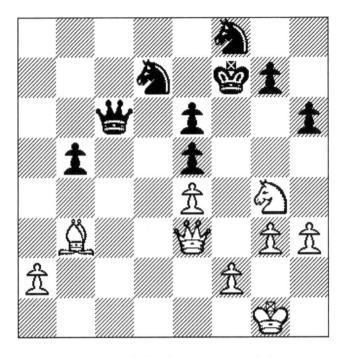

35. Ne5 Ne5 36. Qf4 wins a pawn and the game.
(Fischer-O'Kelly, Buenos Aires 1970)

Black to move

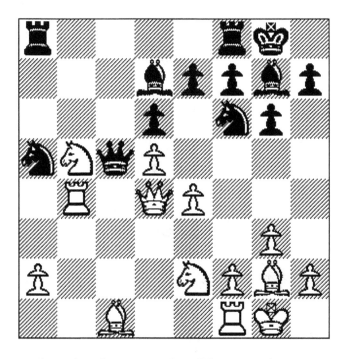

17...Nd5! regains the pawn. The white queen has to move, as attacked by the bishop on g7, but 18. Qd5 Qb4 loses the exchange. After 18. Qc5 dc5 19. Rb1 Nb4 black is much better. (Szabo-Fischer, Buenos Aires 1970)

White to move

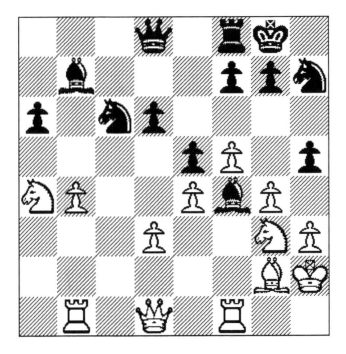

27. Rf4!, black threatens h5-h4, so returning the exchange is the only option, though winning. After 27...ef4 28. Nh5 white has a pawn more, the black f4 and d6 pawns are weak, while the widespread white chains further highlight the advantage.
(Fischer-Garcia, Buenos Aires 1970)

White to move

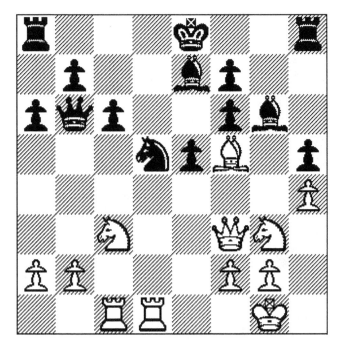

21. Rd5! cd5 22. Nd5 Qd8 23. Rc7 Bd6 24. Rd7 Qd7 25. Nf6
seals it. The alternative capture, 21. Nd5 cd5 22. Rd5 also wins,
but much less convincingly.
(Fischer-Addison, Palma de Mallorca 1970)

98.

Black to move

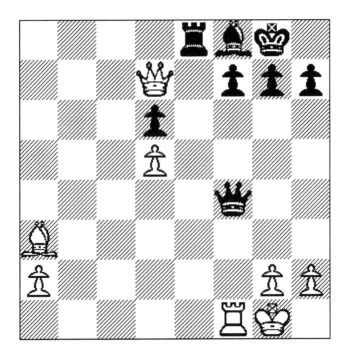

29...Qd4! check, mating. 30. Rf2 Qe1 mate, 30. Kh1 Qf2! 31.
Qb5/Rg1/Ra1 Re1
(Reshevsky-Fischer, Palma de Mallorca 1970)

99.

White to move

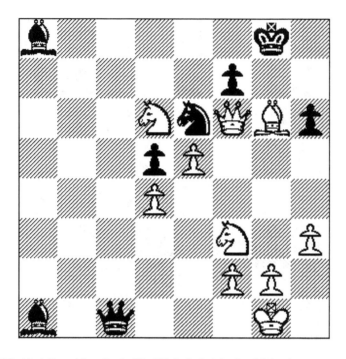

42. Ne1! After 42...Qe1 43. Kh2 fg6 44. Qe6 black gets mated.
42. Kh2 Qf4 check trades queens and no mate in sight.
(Fischer-Ivkov, Palma de Mallorca 1970)

Black to move

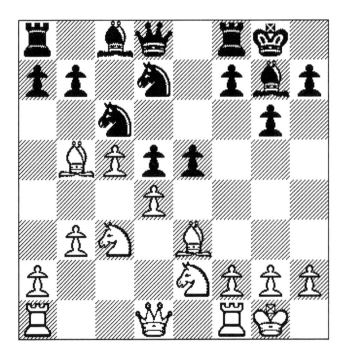

13...Nc5!, now, both after 14. dc5 d4 15. Bd2 dc3 16. Bc3 Be6, and 14. de5 d4 15. Nd4 Ne5 black is bit better. 13...ed4 instead is superior for white, 14. Nd4 Nde5 15. Qd2, and d6 is a good outpost square in certain variations. Such subtleties are frequently important.
(Minic-Fischer, Palma de Mallorca 1970)

Black to move

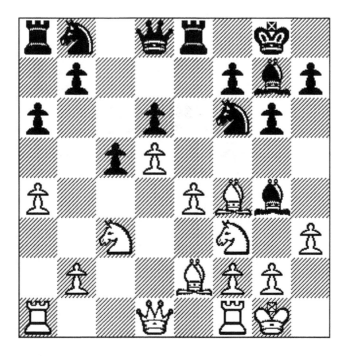

12...Ne4! wins a pawn. 13. hg4 Bc3(14. bc3? Nc3 and Ne2), 13. Ne4 Re4, attacking the undefended bishop on f4, 14. Bg5 Qe8(this time targeting the bishop on e2) 15. Bd3 Bf3 16. Qf3 Rb4. 12...Bf3 13. Bf3 instead leaves white better. (Uhlmann-Fischer, Palma de Mallorca 1970)

White to move

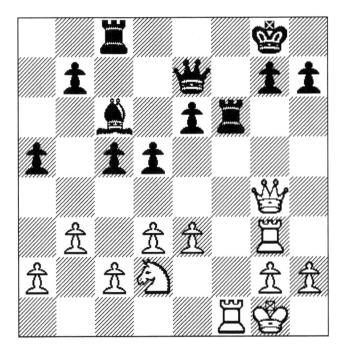

19. Qg7!, wins a pawn. Very simple, very surprising and extremely elegant. 19...Qg7 20. Rf6 and the queen is pinned. Alternative moves like 19. Rf6 and 19. a4 only draw.
(Fischer-Mecking, Palma de Mallorca 1970)

Black to move

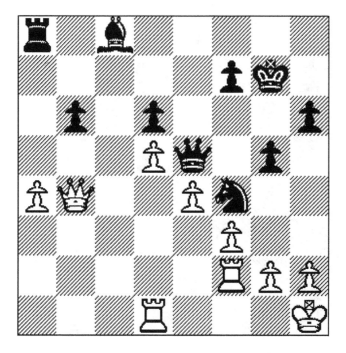

29...Nd3!, forking queen and rook, winning the exchange. 30.
Rd3?? Qa1 mates.
(Fischer-Gligoric, Palma de Mallorca 1970)

104.

Black to move

25...b5!, a paradoxical at first sight move ensures black big advantage, as after 26. cb5(otherwise, black will take on c4 twice) Bb5 27. Nb5(27. Re3 Bd4) Ba1 an exchange is won, and rooks are very strong in the late endgame.
(Ghitescu-Fischer, Rovini-Zagreb 1970)

White to move

35. Rf6!, nice. The queen is lost both after 35...Qf6 36. Nh5 and
35...Kf6 36. Bg5
(Fischer-Gligoric, Rovini-Zagreb 1970)

White to move

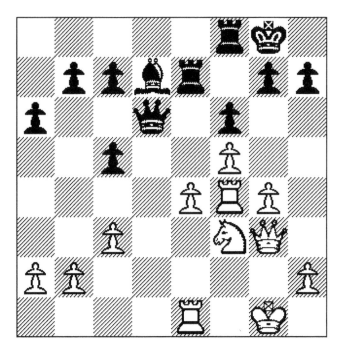

22. e5!, after 22...fe5 23. Rfe4, followed by a capture on e5, instead of the white e4 backward pawn a candidate passer will appear on f5, which certainly is a big positional achievement. Still, if black finds 23...g6!, the game should most probably end in a draw.

(Fischer-Unzicker, Siegen 1970)

White to move

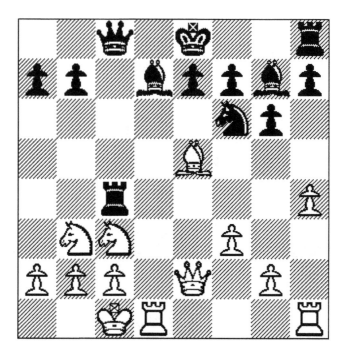

19. Rd7! is an elegant tactical shot. The exchange is sacrificed and black can recapture with 3 different pieces, but all are losing on the spot. 19...Nd7 20. Bg7, 19...Qd7 20. Qc4. If 19...Kd7, then 20. Nb5! and black can not prevent multiple threats, losing significant material, for example, 20...Ke8 21. Bf6, threatening Nd6 queen-forking check, or 20...Rd8 21. Na7 Qa8 22. Qc4 (Fischer-Camara, Siegen 1970)

Black to move

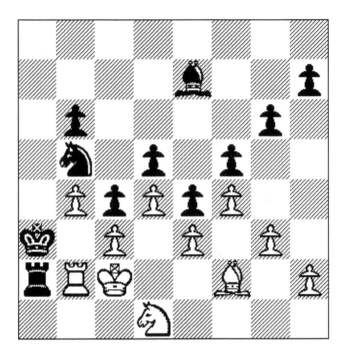

47...Nc3!! 47...Ra1 also wins, but this is way more spectacular and effective. All lines easily lose, 48. Nc3 Rb2, 48. Ra2 Na2, 48. Kc3 Ra1! 49. Kc2 Rd1 50. Kd1 Kb2. 49. Rd2 instead in the last line leads to a sudden and difficult to spot mate in 2 after 49...Rc1 check 50. Rc2 Bb4

(Acevedo-Fischer, Siegen 1970)

White to move

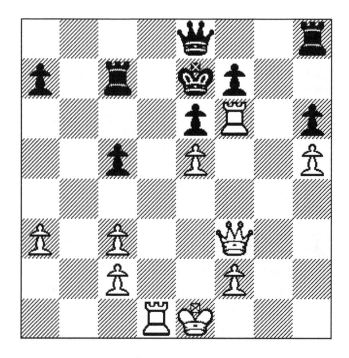

28. Re6, well, this is effective and leads to a forced mate.
28...Ke6/fe6 29. Qf6 mate, 28...Kf8 29. Qf6 Qe6 30. Qh8 Ke7 31.
Qd8 mate.
(Fischer-Hook, Siegen 1970)

110.

Black to move

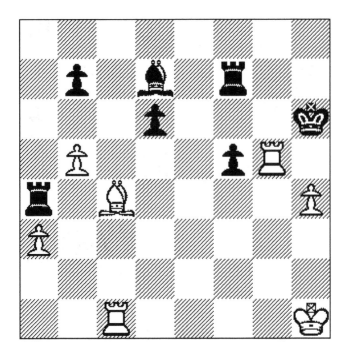

38...Bb5!
39. Bb5? Rh4 check 40. Kg2 Kg5 loses the exchange and two pawns, while 39. Bf7 Rh4 40. Kg2 Kg5 41. Bd5 Rh7 only two pawns.
(Larsen-Fischer, Denver 1971)

Black to move

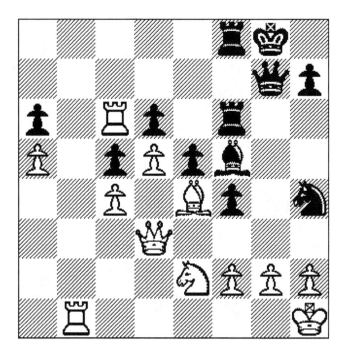

29...f3!, that disrupts the defence of the Be4 upon the g2 square. 30. Bf3 is impossible because the bishop is pinned, while 30. gf3 leads to 30...Qg2 mate. As the knight on e2 is simultaneously attacked, the only line of resistance is 30. Ng3, but then 30...fg2 31. Kg1 Be4 32. Qe4 Nf3 33. Kg2 Nd2 wins in the most convincing of ways.

(Larsen-Fischer, Denver 1971)

Black to move

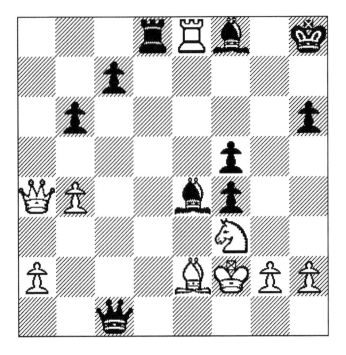

30...Bc6!, forking queen and rook, and winning queen for rook
and minor piece. After 31. Qc6 Qc6 32. Rd8 Kg7 the final
outcome makes no doubt. Other options for white are even worse.
(Taimanov-Fischer, Vancouver 1971)

Black to move

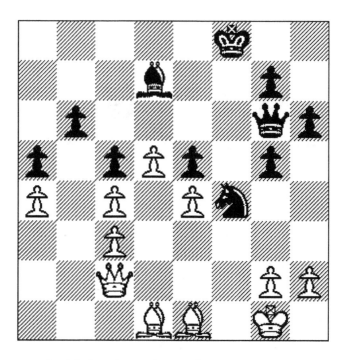

I am certain this has been shown thousands of times, but one
more will not hurt. **27...Ba4!**, so simple and so effective. After 28.
Qa4 Qe4 the black queen simultaneously threatens mate on the g2
and e1 squares, and this threat can only be delayed by a number
of moves. At a cursory glance, the a4 square seems over-
protected, as both the white queen and bishop defend it, but this is
just an optical illusion.
(Spassky-Fischer, Reykjavik 1972)

The positional suite

114.

Black to move

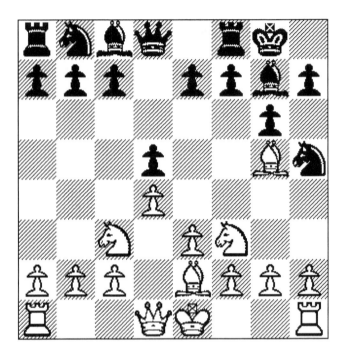

7...h6!, and black gets the bishop pair.
8. Bf4 Nf4, 8. Bh4 g5! 9. Bg3 Ng3
(Bernstein-Fischer, Montreal 1956)

White to move

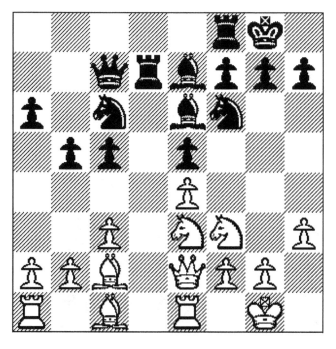

17. Ng5, targeting the bishop on e6 and winning the minor exchange. Bishops are usually significantly more valuable than knights.
(Fischer-Baron, New York 1956)

Black to move

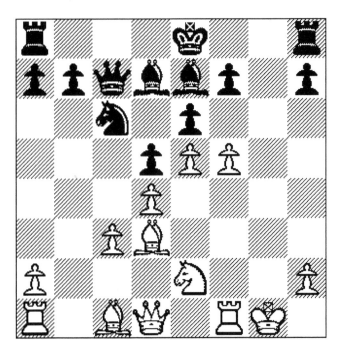

14...gf5!, otherwise, white will play f6 and the black position gets
seriously cramped.
(Tomargo-Fischer, New York 1956)

White to move

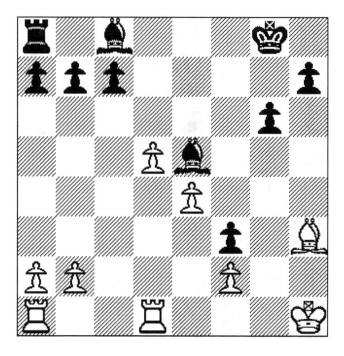

26. Be6!, creating an advanced bishop outpost on the 6th rank, bearing in mind that 26...Be6 27. de6 gives rise to a strong passed pawn on the same square. 26. Bc8 Rc8 instead, only develops the black rook. That is how small positional advantages should be utilised.

(Fischer-Popovych, Oklahoma 1956)

White to move

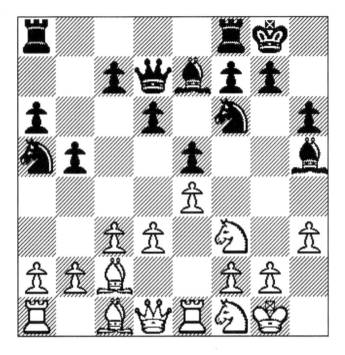

14. g4!, restricting the mobility of the black bishop. In the current situation, this is more important than the weakened white king shelter, as white is attacking.

(Fischer-Di Camillo, Washington 1956)

119.

Black to move

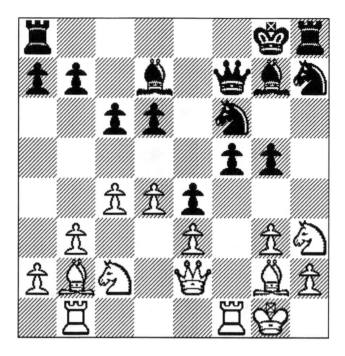

25...g4!, preparing the f3 square for the knight, 26. Nf4 Ng5, and soon the knight will land on f3 with tremendous effect.
(Marchand-Fischer, Washington 1956)

120.

Black to move

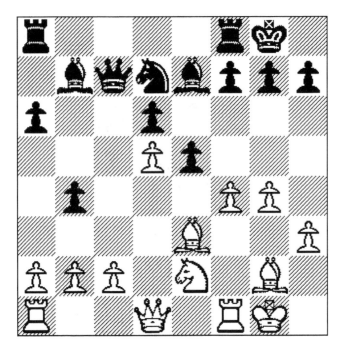

15...ef4!, this prepares the e5 outpost square for the knight. Otherwise, white will play f5 with considerable advantage.
(Garais-Fischer, Cleveland 1957)

White to move

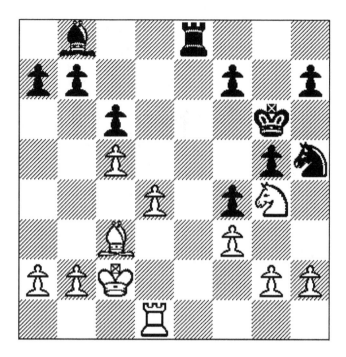

24. d5!, getting rid of the d4 backward pawn. After 24...cd5 25. Rd5, the c5 pawn becomes quite dangerous candidate passer. If 24...Re2, then 25. Kd3, followed by d6, with an easy win. In the case of 24...f5, 25. Nf2 Re2 26. Rd2 Rd2 27. Kd2 cd5 28. Nd3 also wins. Black's main problem is its severely compromised pawn structure on the king side, featuring a symmetrical doubled pawn, which is fully depreciated.
(Fischer-Addison, Cleveland 1956)

Black to move

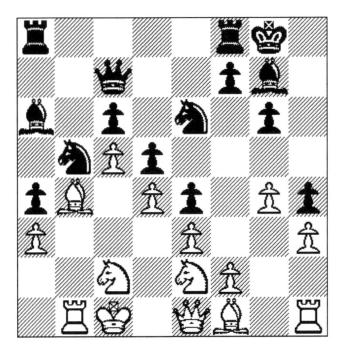

32...f5!, that will open the f file for attack. It is essential to see such more positional than tactical moves.
(Marchand-Fischer, Milwaukee 1957)

White to move

25. g4!, that will avoid opening of the f file for the black rooks, otherwise, black will do so with fg3 and a quick draw after that. If the black rook retreats to g5, it gets trapped and might even be lost at some point.
(Fischer-Green, New Jersey 1957)

White to move

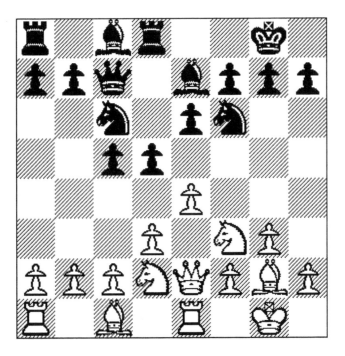

10. e5!, this certainly is the best move. It gains space, tempo and makes the black pawn shelter inflexible. If white does not push e5 now, on the very next move black can simplify the game with de4, with considerably better drawing prospects.
(Fischer-Feuerstein, New York 1957)

White to move

19. a5!, creating a lever, that will open the a file for attack. Levers on advanced ranks are always a good move when attacking. (Fischer-Bisguier, New York 1957)

Black to move

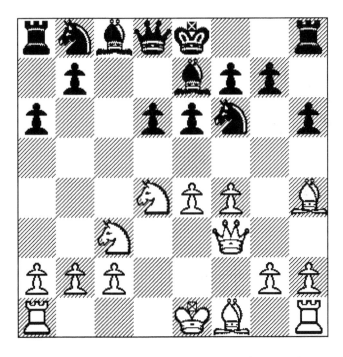

9...g5!!(I like this a lot as a nice positional move, hence the second exclamation mark), removes the f4 pawn from its role of guarding the e5 square, so it becomes an outpost square for the black knight. After 10. fg5 hg5! 11. Bg5 Nbd7 and Ne5, black has fully equal. Fischer played 10...Nfd7, using the pin of the g5 pawn, which can not capture, as the bishop on h4 is hanging, but after 11. Qh5, preventing a capture with the h pawn towards the center, white gets considerably better. Please note, that 9...e5, which is Stockfish's first choice, is nowhere near 9...g5, as after 10. Nf5 Bf5 11. gf5, white retains the pair of bishops and much better attacking prospects.
(Cardoso-Fischer, New York 1957)

White to move

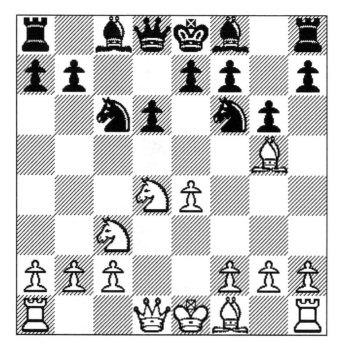

7. Bf6!, this creates a very weak central isolated pawn on d6, as well as an excellent outpost square on d5. The game is close to won, if not altogether won. 7. Bb5 Bd7 and only then Bf6 is way weaker, as the b5 square belongs to the knight, to attack the d6 pawn, and not the bishop.

(Fischer-Bennett, San Francisco 1957)

White to move

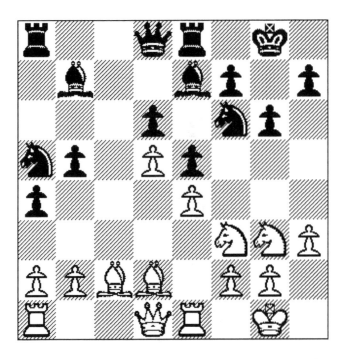

19. b3!, trapping the black knight on a5. Now, the knight can get mobile, only if the black light-square bishop goes to a6, and that is awkward and takes some time. In the process, white should get very active and win some material, probably a pawn. If white does not play b3, then the black knight will go to c4, an excellent advanced location, and then probably, if white plays b3 to expel it, even to a3 or b2. So, this was a very nice, almost obligatory, positional approach. Restricting the mobility of enemy pieces before they get active is a very valid rule in chess.

(Fischer-Sherwin, Bad Portoroz 1958)

Black to move

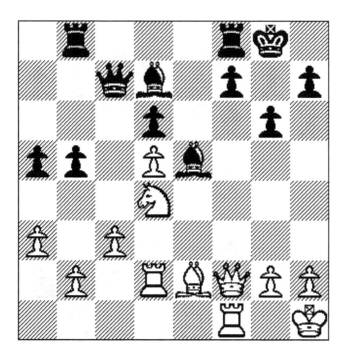

23...b4!, creating an attacking lever that will soon break down the white pawn structure on the queen side. If b4 is not played immediately, then on the very next move white can prevent the threat with Nc2, additionally guarding the b4 square. Such vital moves are not to be missed, as they have strict timing.
(Pilnik-Fischer, Mar del Plata 1959)

White to move

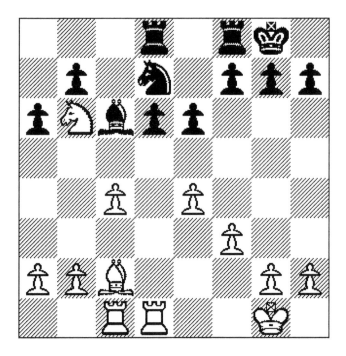

19. Nd5!!(I give 2 exclamation marks here, for the extremely unusual setup). This wins the minor exchange, both after 19...Bd5 20. ed5 and 19...ed5 ed5. Ne7 check and Nb4 with subsequent capture on c6 also threaten. A bishop is usually much stronger than knight in a more open setting, so this excellent trade significantly increases white's winning chances. 19. Nd7 is immeasurably weaker.
(Fischer-Rossetto, Mar del Plata 1959)

White to move

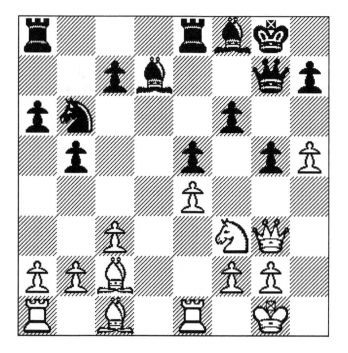

26. Nh2!, targeting the g4 square, and then maybe f5, through e3. Holes are there to be occupied by pieces. At some point, that might win the bishop pair.
(Fischer-Sanchez, Santiago 1959)

White to move

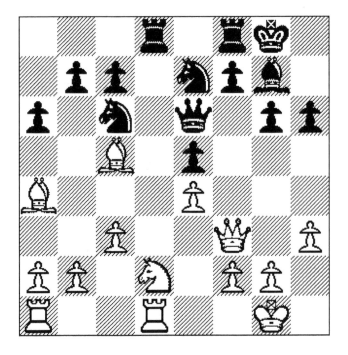

17. Bc6!, creating 3 isolated and a doubled pawn in black's camp after 17...bc6, as 17...Nc6 will lose the exchange on f8. This definitely seals the game.
(Fischer-Stekel, Santiago 1959)

White to move

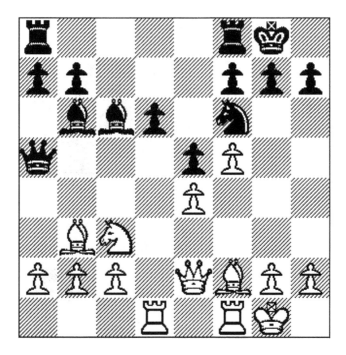

16. g4!, trying to kick the centralised black knight. On 16...h6, 17. h4!, and at some point white will push g5, getting decisive advantage. 16. Rd6? is a mistake, as after 16...Rad8 black gets very active(17. Rad1? Bf2 and black either forks on c5 with the queen or after 18. Qf2 Rd6 19. Rd6 Ng4! 20. Qd2 Qc5 21. Kf1 Nh2 check is much better).

(Fischer-Pilnik, Santiago 1959)

134.

Black to move

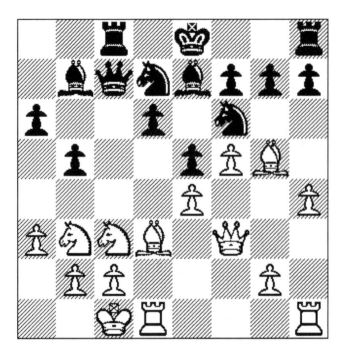

14...h5!, otherwise, white will play g4, and its compact pawns on the king side are very dangerous. At the same time, h5 prepares an excellent outpost square on g4 for the black knight.
(Ader-Fischer, Santiago 1959)

White to move

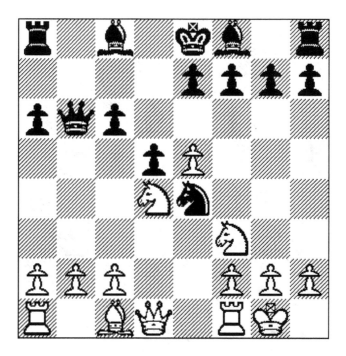

12. e6!, the decisive break, sacrificing a pawn for quick development. After 12...Be6(12...fe6 is even worse) 13. Ne6 fe6 14. Be3!, all white pieces are developed, while the unfortunate doubled e7 and e6 pawns thwart the improvement of black's pieces. White will further take firm control of the e5 square with its minors, open lines for its heavy pieces and win. In case white does not push e6, black will do so on the next move and the game will get about equal.

(Fischer-Olafsson, Yugoslavia 1959)

136.

Black to move

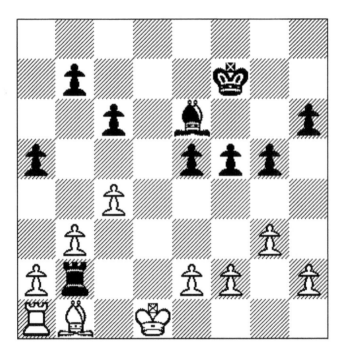

31...a4!, threatening to play a3, and the a3 pawn is extremely strong, while the rook safely protected. White has to capture 32. ba4, after which its pawn structure breaks down badly. Black can capture 32...Bc4, with quite some advantage.
(Donner-Fischer, Zuerich 1959)

White to move

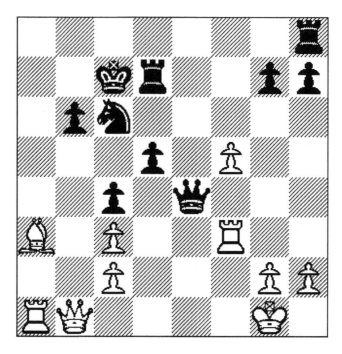

27. Bc1!!(the second exclamation mark is for the subtlety of the move), aiming at f4, to deliver a deadly check, after which Qb5 should decide. Interestingly, a waiting move like 27. h3 leads to a draw after 27...Rf8(targeting f5) 28. Bc1 Rf5 29. Rf5 Qf5 30. Be3 Rb8, while a pseudo-attacking one like 27. Qb5? even loses to 27...Nd4!(a surprise fork) 28. ed4 Qd4 and then Qa1. So that, in similar tactically rich positions, it is extremely important to find the best move. In the present example, 27. Bc1 is a retreat, a paradoxical manoeuver, when you would expect an attacking one, and that makes it so special and difficult to spot.
(Fischer-Darga, Berlin 1960)

138.

White to move

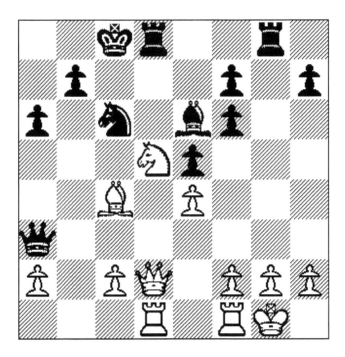

Black threatens Qf3 g3 Bh3. How does white defend? 16. f3 and 16. g3 leave the white shelter too exposed, that should lead to a draw, while 16. Kh1? even loses to 16...Bh3! 17. Rg1 Bg2 18. Rg2 Rg2 19. Kg2 Rg8. **16. Qe3!**, excellent move, after 16...Qe3 17. fe3 the white pawn structure gets completely broken down, 4 isolated pawns, e3, e4, c2 and a2, but that is more than compensated for by the much greater activity of the white pieces and the unpleasant pressure along the f semi-open file. It is now black who has to repel threats(17...Rg4 18. Bd3). Such paradoxical decisions require that all available positional and tactical alternatives are carefully checked beforehand.
(Fischer-Rossetto, Buenos Aires 1960)

White to move

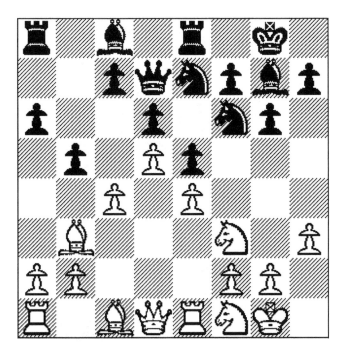

15. c5!, a bit surprising, and strong. Now, 15...dc5 16. Ne5, threatening the queen, trades a central e black for a semi-central c white pawn, increasing the white positional assets and winning chances. If black allows c5-c6, then it is simply cramped and busted. Best chance to defend is probably 15...c6 counter-thrust straight away, and after 16. dc6 Nc6 17. cd6(or 17. Qd6 Qd6 18. cd6), black should recapture the over-extended d6 pawn at some point with decent drawing chances. Moves like c5 are difficult to see, as the pawn goes to an undefended square, and one must figure out the e5 pawn is unprotected after the dc5 capture.
(Fischer-Wade, Buenos Aires 1960)

140.

Black to move

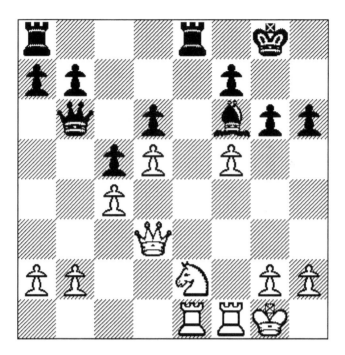

18...g5!, preventing opening of files on the king side. Black should not be afraid of Ng3-h5, as the black bishop has excellent outpost squares on e5 and d4. g5 is a bit counter-intuitive, as this puts another pawn on square the colour of the bishop, making it theoretically bad, but here this is justified, due to the excellent bishop activity, and besides white threatens to win with fg6 and Nf4. So that, each position has its specificities and candidate moves should be carefully investigated.

(Szabo-Fischer, Leipzig 1960)

White to move

23. Qh4!, wrestling over the d open file, as both g7-g5 and f7-f6 are impossible. Whether white wins after 23...Rd4 24. Qd4 is not that important, the important thing is white has chosen the best move, giving it optimal chances. Please note, that 23...Ke8?? now, attempting to defend d8 once more, is a huge tactical blunder due to 24. Bb5! check Bc6 25. Bc6 (Fischer-Pachman, Leipzig 1960)

Black to move

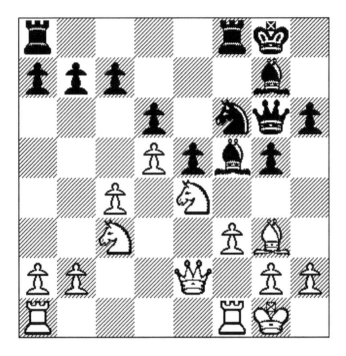

18...g4!, it is important to see that timely attacking break with all the tension in the center with pieces from both camps targeting each other. Sometimes, the complicated tactical conditions make finding such moves difficult.
(Wexler-Fischer, Mar del Plata 1960)

White to move

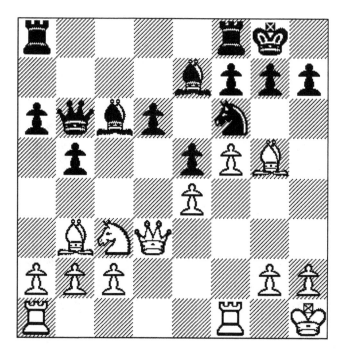

15. Bf6!, trading strong bishop for weak knight, but after 15...Bf6
16. Bd5!(using the fact that the black light-square bishop and
rook on a8 share the same diagonal) Rac8 17. Bc6 Qc6 18. Rf2,
protecting the c2 pawn, followed by Nd5, white gets excellent
knight outpost on d5, the blocked d6 pawn is fully depreciated,
while the black dark-square bishop hemmed in by the central e5
and d6 pawns on squares of same colour. This is already won for
white. It is important to find such good positional moves, just as it
is important to find tactics. The theory that tactics is much more
relevant in a chess game is false, of course, good positional
understanding builds up at least half of what chess is all about.
(Fischer-Gadia, Mar del Plata 1960)

144.

White to move

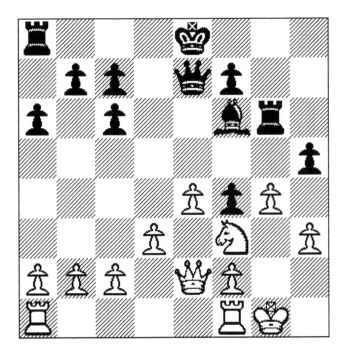

21. g5!, returning the pawn, the white king goes to safety after 21...Bg5 22. Kh2. It is unassailable there, the white pawn center is much stronger and the black f doubled isolated pawns fully depreciated, so white should win that at some point. The alternative, 21. Nh2?, quickly leads to a disaster after 21...hg4 22. hg4 0-0-0, and the white king is too exposed. 22. Ng4 fails to 22...Bb2!(freeing the road to f5 for the f7 pawn) 23. Rb1 f5! 24. Rb2 hg4 25. hg4 Qg7!, targeting both the g4 pawn and the rook on b2.

(Fischer-Alvarez, Mar del Plata 1960)

White to move

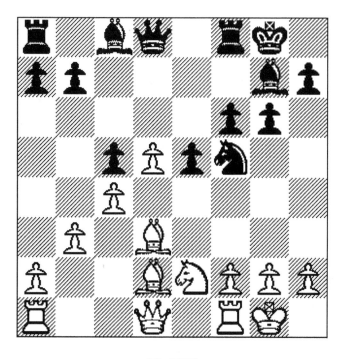

17. Bf5!

The black knight threatens to penetrate on d4, but also in some lines it is an excellent blocker on d6, so trading bishop for knight is the right positional approach. Frequently, a knight outpost on the 5th rank in the center, especially when defended by 2 pawns, as above, is stronger than a bishop, so ceding the bishop pair should not be regrettable. One needs very accurate positional assessment to see such moves, as otherwise, there are no obvious tactics available.
(Fischer-Berliner, New York 1960)

White to move

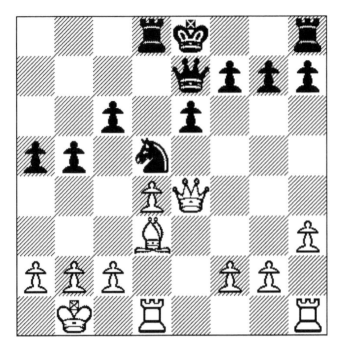

17. c3!, the only way to stop a5-a4. If 17. f4 or 17. Rhe1, 17...a4!, threatening further advance with a3, 18. a3 b4!, and it is already black who is better. Now, on 17...a4, white has 18. a3, binding b4, while on 17...b4, 18. c4, in both cases with some advantage. Miss one such only defensive move, and your advantage not only evaporates, but you might lose the game too.

(Fischer-Petrosian, Bled 1961)

White to move

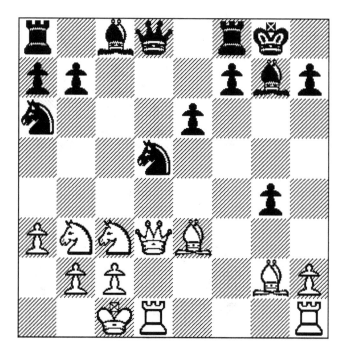

18. h3!, as white is a pawn down, he should try to open files. As now 18...gh3 is suicidal, 18...g3 19. Rhf1 and then Rf3 will win back the g3 pawn at some point with quite some edge. 18. Nd5 ed5 19. Bd5 Qf6 might be even slightly better for black.
(Fischer-Reshevsky, New York 1961)

White to move

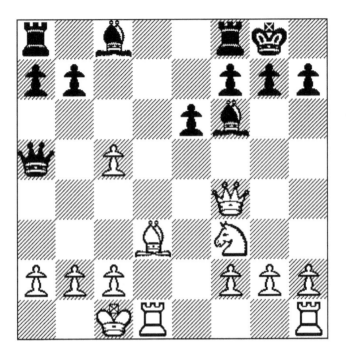

14. Qc4!, protecting simultaneously the c5 and a2 pawns. As 14...b6 15. Qe4, forking the rook on a8 and the h7 square, as well as 14...Bd7 15. Bh7 and Rd7, are both impossible, black will have to lose tempo by playing Be7 to capture the c5 pawn, and this will give decisive advantage to white, who can start a powerful king side attack with h2-h4. 14. Kb1 is much weaker.

(Fischer-Benko, Curacao 1962)

White to move

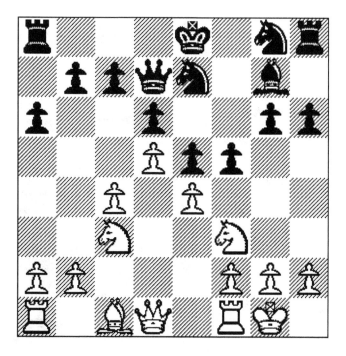

12. ef5! The black king is exposed and that could only be made use of by opening the game. If white misses that opportunity, black will close the game with f5-f4, further threatening a dangerous storm with g6-g5, etc. 12. g3 weakens the white king shelter. This is already deep strategy, one should have played and analysed too many games to know ef5 is the only realistic alternative.

(Fischer-Filip, Curacao 1962)

White to move

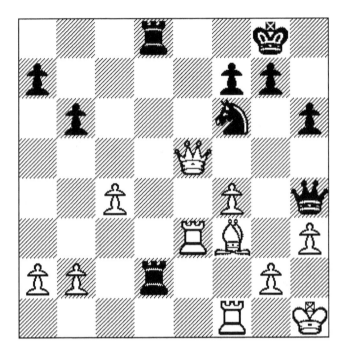

27. b4!, the c passed pawn, after c4-c5, and further c5-c6, safely
supported by the white bishop, should decide the game. 27...Re8
28. Qc3 Qf4 29. Re8 Ne8 30. c5 easily wins
(Fischer-Geller, Curacao 1962)

151.

White to move

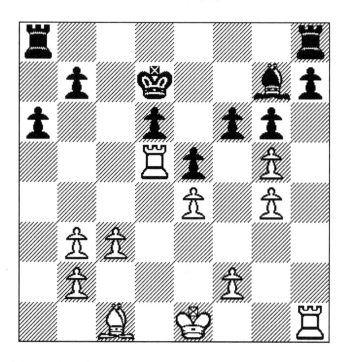

21. gf6!, getting rid of the doubled pawn on the g file, breaking the excellent until now black compact pawn structure on files d through h into 2 separate islands and, after 21...Bf6 22. g5, making the black h7 pawn permanently backward, as the bishop on c1 further controls the h6 push square on an x-ray. Gaining so many relative advantages in a single move, certainly no calculation is required to make this move, just a sound positional evaluation knowledge. After 22. g5, the game is already positionally won for white, taking into account also the weak d5 square. If white chooses instead to follow general endgame principles, activating its king with 21. Ke2, then after 21...fg5! the win is gone, for example 22. Rhd1 Bf8 23. Re5 h6, or 22. Bg5 Rae8 23. c4 h5(instead of backward, the black h pawn is now a passer).

(Fischer-Reshevsky, New York 1962)

Black to move

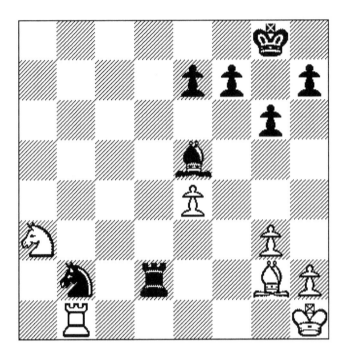

40...h5!, threatening h5-h4, breaking down white's pawns even more after both gh4 and hg3 hg3. Those loose pawns should fall at some point. Again, it is not necessary mo make any calculations, just have a sound positional understanding, assessing isolated pawns in the endgame as big weaknesses.
(Steinmeyer-Fischer, New York 1962)

White to move

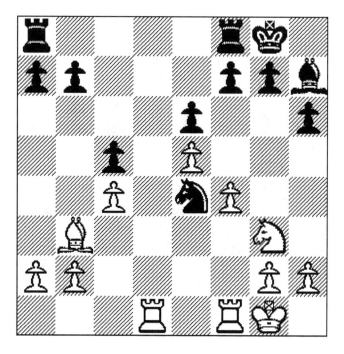

22. Rd7!, sometimes, it is difficult to get the rook to the 7th, make a quiet move, when you have to deal with available trades at the same time. The natural 22. Ne4 Be4 23. Rd7 loses a tempo, as the b7 pawn is already defended by the bishop on e4. Now, although the white pawn structure gets compromised after 22...Ng3 23. hg3, the h pawn has captured towards the center and after 23...Be4 24. Ba4 Rad8 25. Rfd1, white is in full control of the 7th rank, as well as the d file, and most probably should win at some point.

(Fischer-Portisch, Stockholm 1962)

White to move

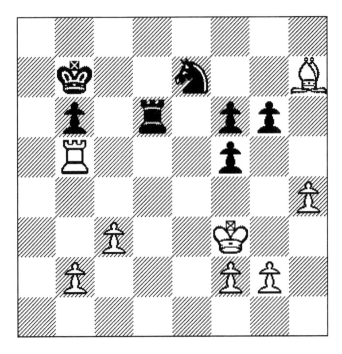

49. h5!, breaking down the black pawn structure into 3 isolated
pawns after 49...gh5(49...Ka6 50. c4) 50. Bf5, significantly
facilitating the win.
(Fischer-Barcza, Stockholm 1962)

White to move

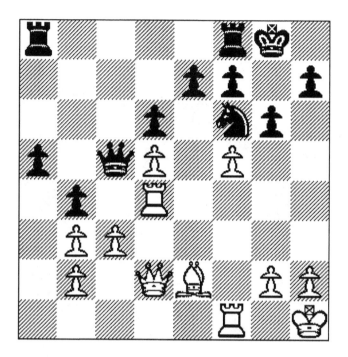

22. Bc4!, on c4, the bishop is semi-outposted, the enemy d6 pawn can not realistically attack it, as it is blocked, protects the d5 pawn and is itself nicely protected. Psychologically, this move is difficult to see, though, as the friendly b3 and d5 pawns create the illusion the bishop is hemmed in there, and useless. After 22...bc3 23. bc3 a4 24. b4!, white gets considerable advantage.
(Fischer-Schweber, Stockholm 1962)

White to move

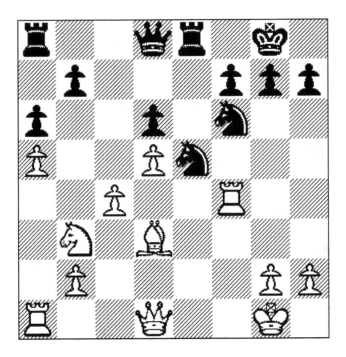

19...b6!, getting rid of the b7 backward pawn on time and binding the c4 pawn. Black threatens to take control of the b semi-open file after Rb8. Such backward pawns are to be eliminated, even if isolated pawns like a6 are created in the process, as the opened files give sufficient counterplay. In case black makes a waiting move like 19...Qc7, white gets fully equal after 20. Nd4.
(Yanofsky-Fischer, Stockholm 1962)

White to move

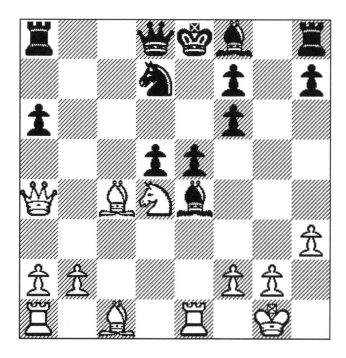

14. Re4!!, the second exclamation mark is for the elegance of the solution. This is the only winning move. It might seem to someone one will need an engine to be certain of the right move, but that is definitely not so, one should simply calculate the positional consequences of each candidate move to pick the best. After 14. Re4 dc4 15. Nf5!(the bishop is gone and does not control the f5 square any more), or 14...de4 15. Nf5!, white gets at least the bishop pair for the exchange, the d file gets opened and the black king is further weakened, so this is more than sufficient compensation for the material deficit. It is really not necessary to calculate all the consequences of the sacrifice: it should be sound, as white gets too many relative advantages in return. So, this is more a positional than a tactical sacrifice. It is important to note that Re4 also pins the black e5 pawn, so the ed4 capture is impossible. In case white plays some random move, like 14. a3, for example, then after 14...Bg2! 15. Kg2 dc4 black has almost fully equalised, as the white king is weak too. 14. Bf1 will fail to 14...ed4 15. f3 f5 16. fe4 de4 17. Bf4 Bg7, and black is in perfect condition.

(Fischer-Najdorf, Varna 1962)

158.

White to move

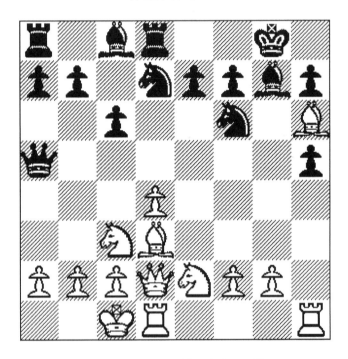

13. g4!, that will open the g or h file, it is really not necessary to calculate any further, bearing in mind white's enormous development lead.

(Fischer-Robatsch, Varna 1962)

Black to move

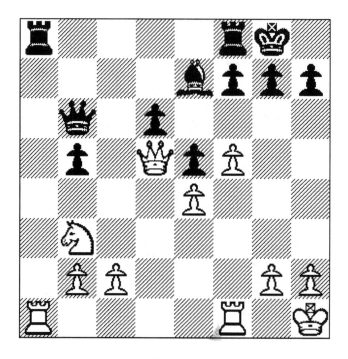

19...Ra4!
As capturing on a4 is impossible, because of the weak b2 pawn,
black can further try to take control of the a file, for example after
20. c3 Qa6!, and further penetrate to the 7th rank with Ra2. This
will leave black good winning chances, at least quite some
pressure. If Ra4 is not played, then after, for example,
19...Rac8(the rook should leave the a8 square, where it is twice
attacked) 20. c3 b4 21. c4 Bg5 22. Nd2!, and further Nf3, the
position is very close to fully equal(22...Bd2 23. Qd2 Rc4 24.
f6!).
(Unzicker-Fischer, Varna 1962)

Black to move

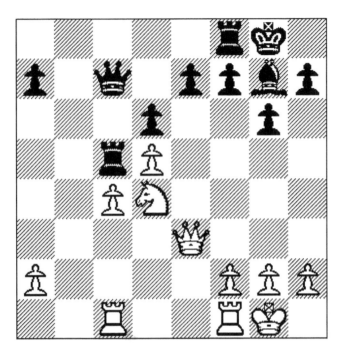

21...Bd4!, otherwise, the knight will penetrate to c6, and it is already white who is a bit better. This is a case when a stronger bishop is sacrificed for a weaker knight, so that the knight does not become stronger.
(Blau-Fischer, Varna 1962)

Black to move

20...a6!, otherwise, if white plays a6 instead, the white space cramp on the queen side becomes too weighty after black responds with b6(or the a file gets opened). This might definitely have a bearing upon the final result of the game. The 20...a6 move is a purely positional one, taking into account space considerations. In 90% of cases such moves should be made automatically, as a pawn on the 6th rank is significantly stronger than a pawn on the 5th rank.

(Bisguier-Fischer, Bay City 1963)

Black to move

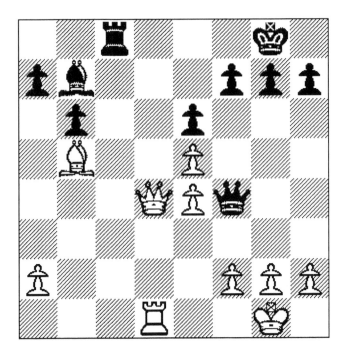

20...g5!, getting rid of the possible back rank mate and threatening Qe4. On 21. Re1, 21...Rc5 is quite strong, if 21. f3, then 21...g4! creates a powerful storming pawn, where fg4 leaves the e4 central pawn undefended. 21. Bd3 might draw the game, though. Alternatives like 20...h6 are much weaker, as they objectively pose significantly less problems to white.
(Berliner-Fischer, Bay City 1963)

Black to move

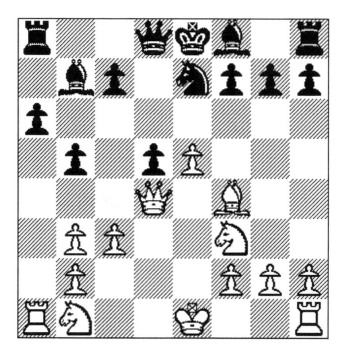

11...c5!, one more elegant stroke, making use of the fact that 12. Qc5?? Nf5 traps the queens, and black wins at least a piece after 13. Bg5 Bc5 14. Bd8 Rd8. The move simultaneously gains tempo and significantly improves black's pawn structure. 11...Nf5 12. Qd3 leaves white better. Miss a player one such subtlety, and he already gets worse instead of legitimately getting better.
(Addison-Fischer, New York 1963)

164.

White to move

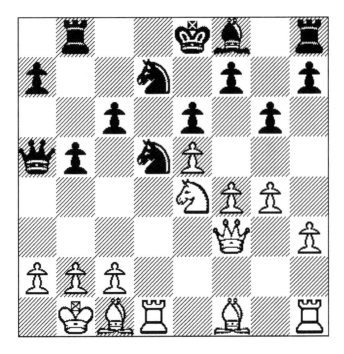

16. f5!, there are other winning moves, but that one is the most straightforward. When considerably up in development, try opening the game, even at the cost of material, so this break is by far the most natural. It is not necessary to calculate any variations at that, they might be too long and not fully forced, because this is simply a positional sacrifice.

(Fischer-Beach, Poughskeepsie 1963)

White to move

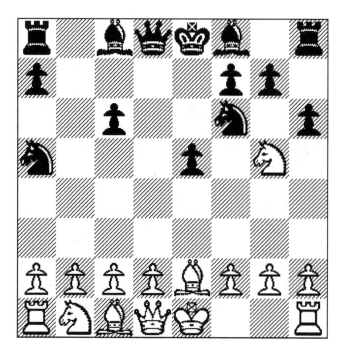

9. Nh3! 9. Nf3 e4 gains black too many development tempos and sets a powerful central pawn on e4, so simply compromise your pawn structure after Bh3 gh3, get the bishop pair and develop as quickly as possible. The move might be theoretical in a sense, but is well worth it. This might be one of the reasons the Two Knights Opening, from which above position arose, is altogether lost for black.

(Fischer-Bisguier, Poughskeepsie 1963)

White to move

22. Bg3!, preparing f2-f4 and e4-e5. Winning or not, this is the only realistic winning attempt for white, so should be tried. Sometimes, it is difficult to find retreating manoeuvers when attacking, but here the bishop should step back to allow the f pawn to move forward.

(Fischer-Szabo, Havana 1965)

White to move

16. gf3!, severely compromising the white pawn structure, but opening the g file for attack. After 16...Qd7 17. Rdg1 f6 18. Rg7! Qg7 19. Rg7 Kg7 20. Qf4 white should win the arisen ending, as the black king is too exposed and some more black pawns will fall. 16. Rf3 instead is easily very drawish after 16...Qd7 17. g4 Qd5
(Fischer-Bilek, Havana 1965)

White to move

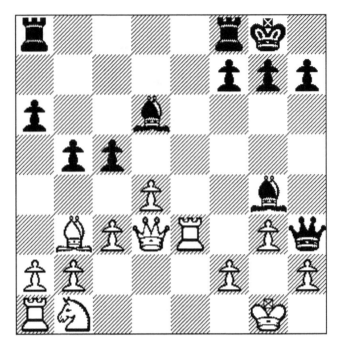

18. Bd5!, gaining tempo and getting the bishop to the king side, where it will nicely defend the own king. After 18...Rad8 19. Nd2 Bc7 20. Bg2 Qh5 21. d5 white gets quite some edge. This is a typical manoeuver in the Marshall, ensuring white much better chances.

(Fischer-Donner, Havana 1965)

White to move

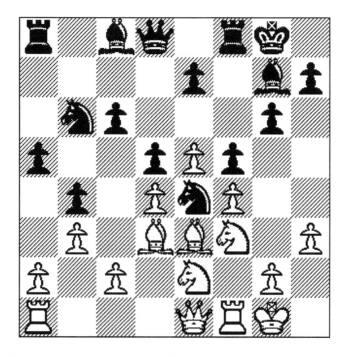

15. a3!, the backward a2 pawn is gone, and after ab4 ab4, or ba3
Ra3 either the b4 or a5 black pawns become weak.
Psychologically, it is difficult to sometimes see such moves
easily, as, usually, one is expected to play on the part of the board
where one is strong, and that would be the king side for white
now, but the matter of fact is there are no useful moves for white
on the king side now. So that, another useful principle to check is:
"Try to improve not only where you are stronger, but also where
you are weaker".
(Fischer-Suttles, New York 1965)

Black to move

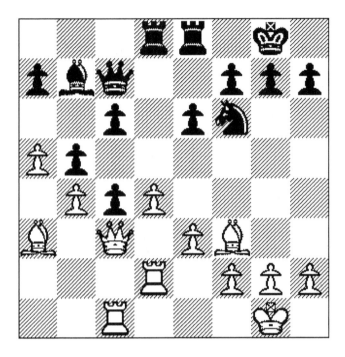

20...c5!
21. dc5 Rd2 22. Qd2 Bf3 23. gf3 Rd8 and Rd3 should be
sufficient for a win, 21. bc5? loses even quicker to 21...Bf3 22.
gf3 Rd5!, aiming at h5, while 21. Bb7 fails to 21...cd4 and then
Qb7. 20...a6 also wins, but this, paradoxical at first sight, counter-
break, is more straightforward. Finding the move is not so much
related to a tactical solution, rather than a positional one, black
gets rid of its bad bishop, even at the cost of a pawn.
(Evans-Fischer, New York 1965)

White to move

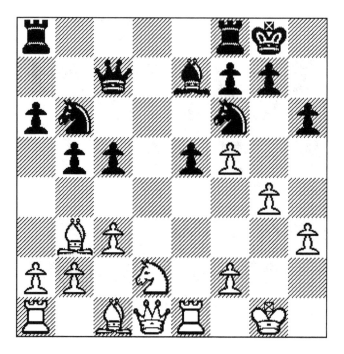

17. h4!, white threatens g4-g5. After 17...c4 18. Bc2 Nfd5 19.
Nf3 and g5 white has crushing advantage. Funnily, Stockfish does
not see that line. It is not counter-indicative to move pawns from
your shelter, when such dangerous storming pawns are created.
Quite the opposite, frequently, this is the best strategy.
(Fischer-Benko, New York 1965)

White to move

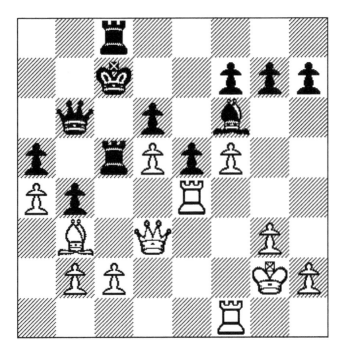

27. Bc4!, the bishop heads to b5, and then c6, where it will become much more powerful outpost and much more attacking. This will win the game at some point for white. Quite frequently, tactics play only secondary role, it is important to find moves that gradually improve your positional assets.

(Fischer-Zuckerman, New York 1965)

White to move

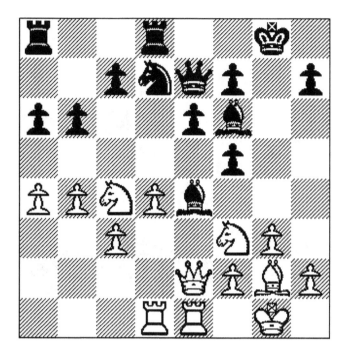

19. g4!!, the two exclamation marks are because probably this is the only winning move. White threatens to compromise black's pawn structure beyond repair after gf5 gf5, or to win material after gf5 Bf5 Nfe5. 19...Bf3 20. Bf3 Rb8 21. gf5 is even worse. 19...Rb8 20. gf5 Bf5 21. Nfe5 Be5 22. Ne5 Ne5 23. Qe5 also leaves white with substantial edge. One more move Stockfish does not see of the later Fischer.
(Fischer-Minev, Havana 1966)

Black to move

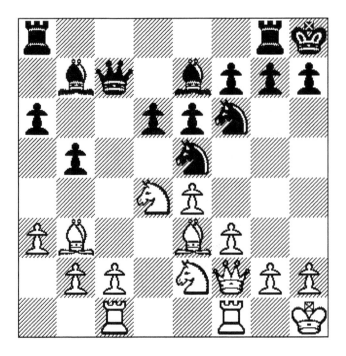

16...g5!, threatening g5-g4 and Rg8-g6(to later play Ra8-g8), while making the e5 knight semi-outposted. 16...d5 or 16...Nc4 are hardly better.
(Soruco-Fischer, Havana 1966)

White to move

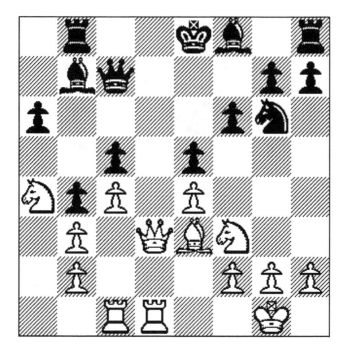

18. Nb6!, as 18...Qb6 is impossible because of 19. Qd7 mate, this will send a powerful knight on d5 on the next move. Thus, using tactics, the otherwise weak rim knight on a4 suddenly becomes central and powerful.

(Fischer-Johannessen, Havana 1966)

176.

White to move

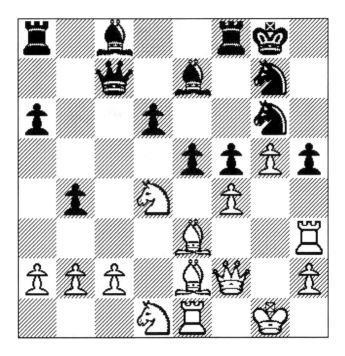

25. Bh5!, of course, the white knight does not need to go anywhere, white just needs to open the h file for attack. After 25...Nh5(the knight on g6 is threatened) 26. Rh5 ed4 27. Bd4 Bb7 28. Rh6 the win is really simple.

(Fischer-Saidy, New York 1966)

Black to move

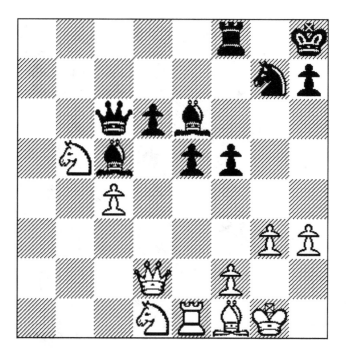

Are the pawns equal? No, although the count is same, black leads at least by a full pawn in material, as its pawns are much more central. **34...f4!**, starting a ferocious assault on the king side. After 35. g4 h5! 36. Bg2 Qd7, black is close to winning.
(Rossolimo-Fischer, New York 1966)

178.

Black to move

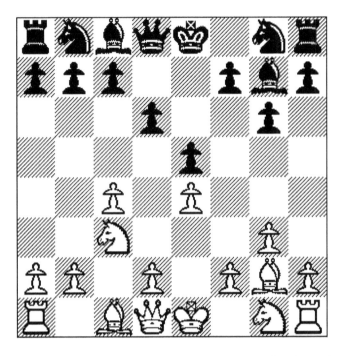

5...f5!, of course, after 6. ef5 gf5! 7. Qh5 Kf8 and Nf6, only black could have the advantage due to its superior central pawn structure. Stockfish does not think so, though, as usual, it does not see anything that is longer than 5 moves.

(Byrne-Fischer, New York 1966)

Black to move

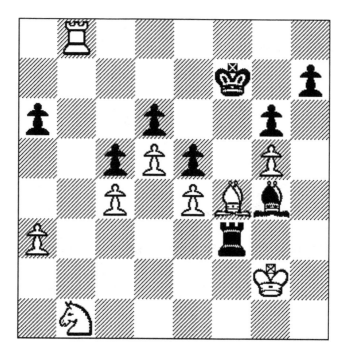

46...ef4!, of course, creating a passed pawn is the much stronger move. 46...Rf4 47. Nd2 could even end in a draw. Sometimes, creating a passed pawn after a capture is difficult to recognise for a human, as he is concentrated on the capturing property. When possible, always create passed pawns, they will largely paralyse the opponent's resources.

(Sherwin-Fischer, New York 1966)

180.

Black to move

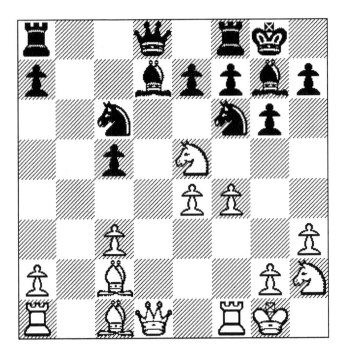

15...Ne5!, after 16. fe5 Ne8 and Nc7 the e5 doubled isolated pawn is extremely weak and should fall at some point. That will give black good winning chances.
(Bisguier-Fischer, New York 1966)

Black to move

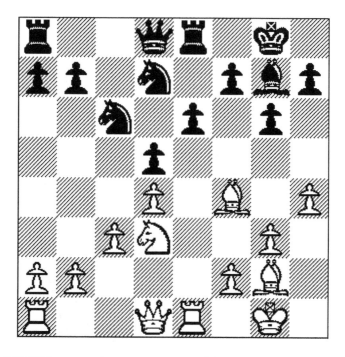

19...h5! This move is necessary, positionally. If black does not play h5, then white will do so himself, and after hg6 hg6 Bf3, Kg2 and Rh1 open and use the h file for attack. A good rule of thumb might be to answer h2-h4 with h7-h5, whenever your king is on the king side. In this way, you will prevent enemy pawn storms that are much more dangerous than weakening a bit the shelter. This rule might not always be true, but will hold in 90% of cases.

(Ivkov-Fischer, Santa Monica 1966)

White to move

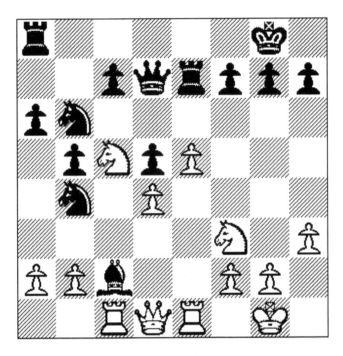

20. Qd2! 20. Rc2 captures just the bad black bishop, and white wants to take the good knight on b4 with the opponent light-square bishop staying alive. After 20...Qe8 21. Qb4 white enjoys much bigger positional advantage in comparison to the bishop capture. Again, this is a purely positional move.
(Fischer-Reshevsky, Santa Monica 1966)

Black to move

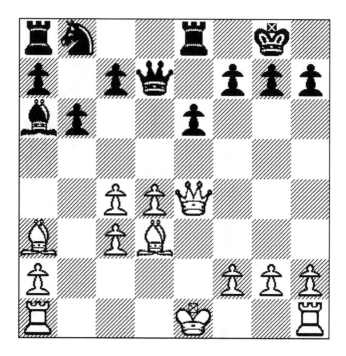

White has forked the a8 rook and the h7 shelter square. **13...f5!** is the bold and very powerful reply. After 14. Qa8 Nc6 15. Qe8 Qe8 16. 0-0 Na5, followed by a bishop capture on c4, black trades light-square bishops, remaining with a pawn more, good knight outpost on c4 and more compact pawn structure. The assessment should be close to winning. If 14. Qe2 instead, then again Nc6-a5 leaves black much better. Again, this is a purely positional move/sacrifice, though some tactics should be figured out to be certain how it goes.

(Portisch-Fischer, Santa Monica 1966)

White to move

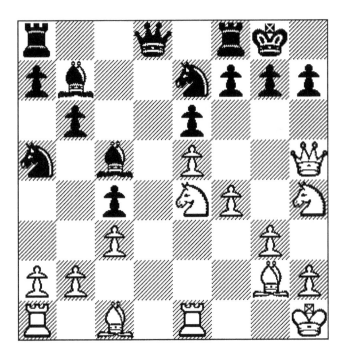

17. g4!, threatening to continue the assault with f4-f5, opening the black king position or wedging on f6. After 17...Ng6 18. Nf3, the f5 threat is still there, while 18...Be4 19. Re4 is not a better alternative. If necessary, white can even play Qh3-g3 and then h4, to strengthen the assault. It is always good to create such advanced pawn masses, especially on the side where the enemy king is. Stockfish does not see that move too. Clearly, at his best, Fischer has been regularly outplaying Stockfish.
(Fischer-Ivkov, Santa Monica 1966)

Black to move

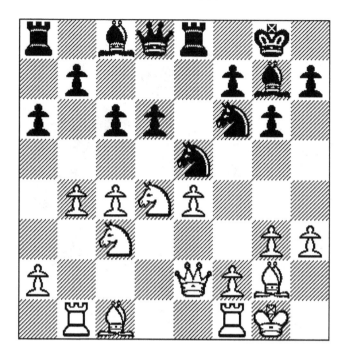

13...b5!, creating a powerful knight outpost square on c4. After 14. cb5 cb5, followed by Nc4, it is difficult to challenge the c4 knight, and this will gain black some tempos and initiative. The only way for white to prevent that setup is to play 15. a4, but then, after 15...ba4 16. Na4 Bd7 17. Qd1 Nc6(attacking the e4 pawn) black gets quite some edge. Another instance of a purely positional decision.
(Donner-Fischer, Santa Monica 1966)

Black to move

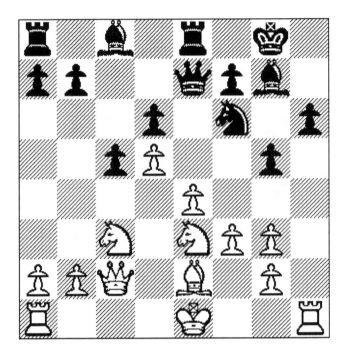

19...Nh7!, the knight heads to e5, via f8 and g6. 19...Nd7, with
the same aim, fails to 20. Nf5, as the c8 bishop does not guard the
f5 square any more. Improving the positioning of one's pieces is
one of the most important aspects of good chess play, especially
in positions of more closed/manoeuvering character as the one
above. Fail to do that and go for a more direct approach, and you
are frequently choosing a suboptimal strategy.
(Larsen-Fischer, Santa Monica 1966)

White to move

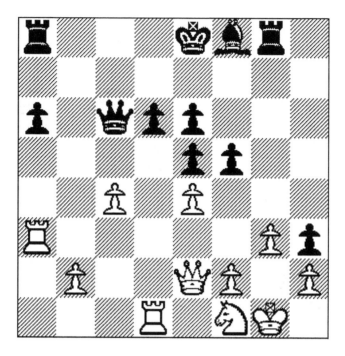

26. c5!(26. Qh5 check, and only then c5, is identical), breaking open the black king position. Accepting the pawn loses easily, after either 26...dc5 27. Qh5 and Ne3, or 26...Qc5 27. Qh5 and Rc3. cd6 also threatens. The only way to avoid immediate disaster seems to be 26...Qe4, but then 27. Qh5, followed by Ne3, easily wins. Even taking on e4 with the queen, 27. Qe4 fe4 28. cd6 should be sufficient for a win, as all of black's pawns are isolated and easy prey for the enemy pieces. Please note, that white can even lose this game, if it decides to take on f5, 26. ef5, as Qg2 mates.

(Fischer-Najdorf, Santa Monica 1966)

White to move

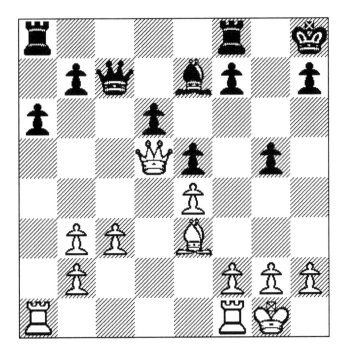

19. Ra4!, aiming at Rb4, and then targeting the b6 square, either with the rook or the bishop. Gaining space advantage, either with pawns or pieces, is always a welcome strategy. On 19...b5, white has 20. Ra2 and then Rfa1, and the a6 pawn is rather weak. 19. b4 should be weaker, although still winning.

(Fischer-Badilles, Meralco 1967)

White to move

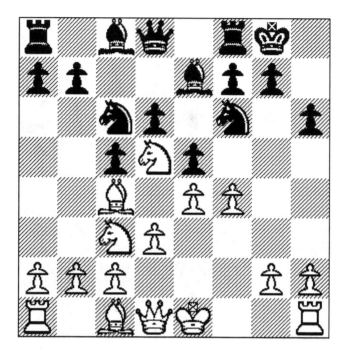

9. f5!, closing the game and threatening an inevitable pawn storm on the king side is certainly the best strategy.
(Fischer-Naranja, Meralco 1967)

White to move

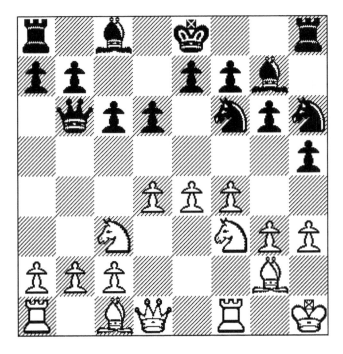

12. Nh4!, threatening both f5 and e5, depending on what black chooses to do. Sometimes, such best moves on the edge of the board are difficult to see.

(Fischer-Vister, Meralco 1967)

Black to move

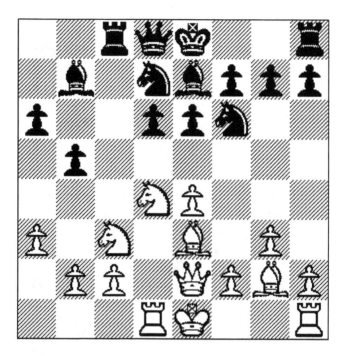

12...Rc3! This is a standard sacrifice in the Sicilian. After 13. bc3 Ne4 14. Be4 Be4 15. 0-0 Qa8, black gets the bishop pair plus pawn, with the white pawn structure severely compromised, more than sufficient compensation, and is close to winning. 14. Rd3 Nc3! and 14. Qd3 Ne5 are even weaker.

(Reyes-Fischer, Meralco 1967)

Black to move

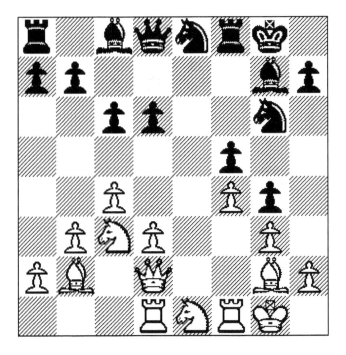

18...h5!, h5-h4-h3 will create tremendous cramp on the king side, already giving black a winning position. All one needs to find this is to assess properly space advantage. Space, especially on the king side, the side where the enemy king is, is essential.
(Lombardy-Fischer, Monaco 1967)

Black to move

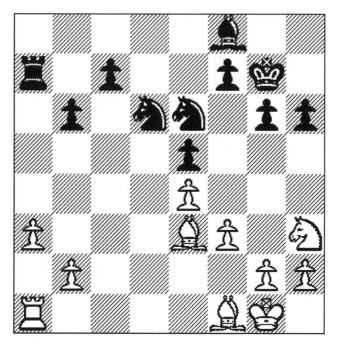

25...Nb7!, the best move, associated with a retreat. This threatens to change bishops on c5, getting rid of the opponent bishop pair. After the trade, white will stay with a relatively bad light-square bishop due to the blocked central e4 pawn on square of its colour. White can not avoid the trade, as, in case the bishop on e3 leaves the g1-a7 diagonal, for example after 26. Bd2, black will continue with Bc5-d4, creating an even stronger outpost, which should be changed at some point one way or another. 26. b4 is impossible, because of Bb4. Again, a purely positional motif.

(Larsen-Fischer, Monaco 1967)

Black to move

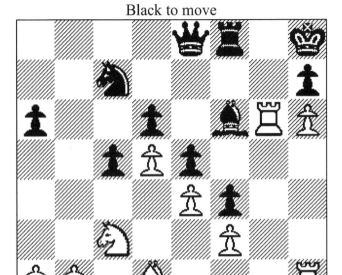

Black should recapture on g6. To someone, it might seem as there is no distinction between the 2 possible captures, with the queen and the pawn, and others might even prefer Qg6 as this develops the queen, but all that is too superficial. In case of a Qg6 capture, the game will most likely end in a draw, as neither side has sufficient relative advantages to claim the win and the white h6 pawn is very strong. **32...hg6!**, excellent move. Black improves its pawn structure significantly, as the former isolated h7 pawn is now not such, and instead it has joined a larger group of friendly pawns spanning files c through g. At some point, g6-g5-g4 thrust will threaten, creating a dangerous passed pawn on the f file. Now, the white h pawn becomes weak and vulnerable, as it will be safely blocked by the black king and easily attackable by the black forces. How many relative advantages with a single humble pawn move are achieved! After the pawn recapture, black retains very good winning chances.

(Gligoric-Fischer, Monaco 1967)

Black to move

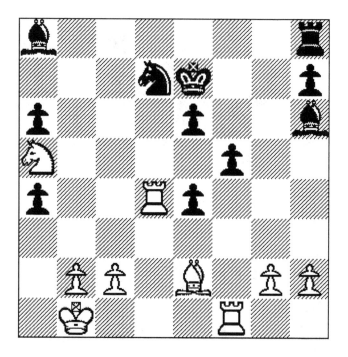

26...a3!, that will break down white's pawn structure after a possible ba3 capture, set up a powerful advanced passer, in case white passes with b2-b3 or b2-b4, or win a pawn after ab2. Obviously, by far the best move, further increasing black's winning chances.

(Minic-Fischer, Skopje 1967)

Black to move

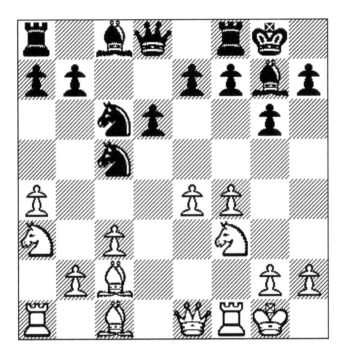

12...Nb3! This wins one of the white bishops, leaving the bishops pair for black(13. Bb3 Qb6 check and Qb3). 12...Qb6 13. Kh1 Nb3 14. Be3(or Nc4) is not equivalent, the latter winning for white.

(Maric-Fischer, Skopje 1967)

White to move

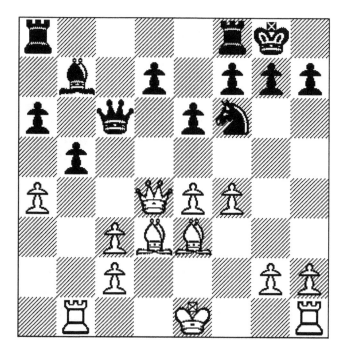

14. Rb4! An elegant way to defend the e4 pawn. 14. ab5 ab5 only opens the a file for black, giving it better chances. After 14...d5 15. e5 Ne4 16. 0-0 white retains some advantage.
(Fischer-Matulovic, Skopje 1967)

White to move

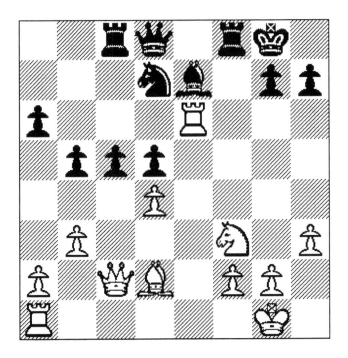

22. Ba5! After 22...Qa5 23. Re7(the rook is already to the 7th) cd4 24. Qe2 Nf6 25. Qe6 white enjoys quite some edge. 22...Qe8? 23. Qe2 Rf7 24. Ng5 loses on the spot. Stockfish prefers 22. Ra6, which is definitely weaker and might easily end in a draw.
(Fischer-Barczay, Sousse 1967)

White to move

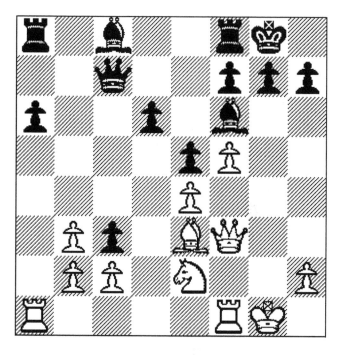

How should white recapture on c3? 18. Nc3 certainly leaves
white much better, with decent winning chances, but **18. bc3!** is
the incomparably superior solution. The b pawn becomes more
central c pawn, and, on the very next move, white can play c3-c4,
with a deadly bind upon the d6 black pawn. No doubt this is
winning for white. The decision one has to take here is a purely
positional one.
(Fischer-Hamann, Nathania 1968)

200.

Black to move

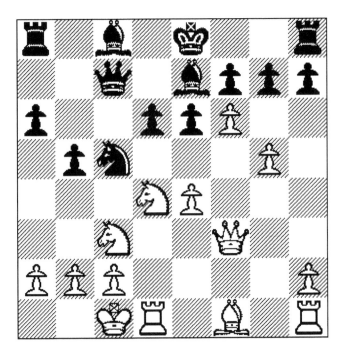

14...gf6! After 15. gf6 Bf8 black has some minimal advantage.
This is a defensive resource, as otherwise, after 14...Bf8? 15.
Bb5! check ab5 16. Ndb5, followed by fg7 and a knight capture
on d6, white is winning.
(Ciocaltea-Fischer, Nathania 1968)

White to move

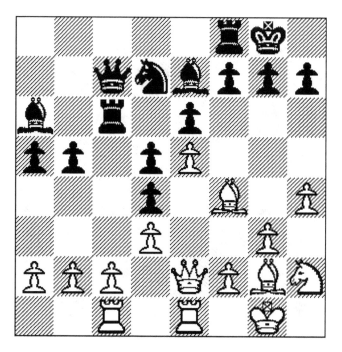

17. Bd5!, another elegant shot. After 17...ed5 two doubled
isolated pawns on the d file are created for black, which are
extremely weak. Both 18. e6 Bd6 19. Bd6 Qd6 20. ed7 Qd7 21.
Nf3, and 18. e6 Qd8 19. ed7 Re6 20. Qg4 Qd7(20...f5 should boil
down to the same) 21. Re6 Qe6 22. Qe6 fe6 23. Re1 are hopeless,
as the d4 pawn is too weak, while the white pawn structure much
superior. The best option for black might be to decline
recapturing with 17...Rc5!, which after 18. Be4 Rc8(counter-
attack on c2) 19. Nf3 Rc2 20. Rc2 Qc2 21. Nd4 leaves some
saving chances due to the fact that the central d3 pawn is
backward. If you ask me, this is a purely positional approach
move, as white does not gain material in the process, with the key
point being the creation of two extremely weak doubled isolated
pawns on the d file.
(Fischer-Geller, Nathania 1968)

202.

Black to move

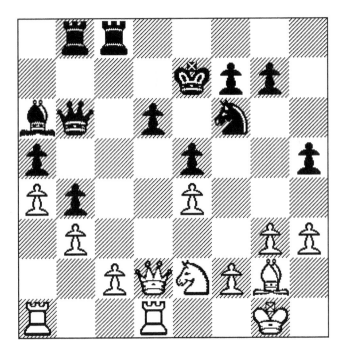

21...Be2!, after that move, the black rook penetrates on c3, and black gets good knight for bad bishop(especially the e4 white central pawn is blocked on square the colour of the bishop), more than sufficient reasons to trade an otherwise stronger bishop.
(Matulovic-Fischer, Vinkovci 1968)

White to move

22. Bc7!, as 22...Re1 23. Re1 Qc7 24. Re8 check Nf8 25. Qb4 Be7 26. Re7 loses a piece and the game, black has to opt for 23...Qf8 24. Ne4, threatening both Nd6 and d6, with quite some white advantage, most probably winning. For me, this is a positional decision, as Bc7, later followed by occupation of the d6 square by a pawn or knight, improves the overall piece positioning of the white pieces, and gaining space is always welcome. No obvious tactical material gain.
(Fischer-Matanovic, Vinkovci 1968)

Black to move

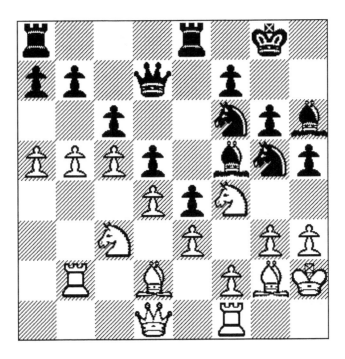

19...Bg4!! Tremendous move Stockfish will not see even after hours. There is not forced mate in all lines and the material gain at the end of a very long line is difficult to see, but one does not need to do all that to play the move. After 20. hg4 hg4, black opens the h file for its heavy pieces, while the f2 shelter pawn becomes permanently backward, which will spell doom for the white king at some point. To know why Bg4 is the best move, one should study the outlines of the position, rather than make very deep calculations. Recognising specific winning patterns is a powerful approach.
(Nicolic-Fischer, Vinkovci 1968)

White to move

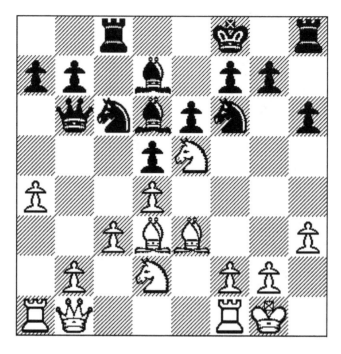

18. f4!, a strong move, the e5 knight is now twice defended and very powerful, irremovable, and white threatens to push f4-f5 at any time. Again, the lines can not be exhausted tactically, this is a purely positional decision. Stockfish for some reason does not see that move. 18.Nd7 would be more like a positional mistake, as the black light-square bishop is rather weak, hemmed in by friendly pawns.

(Fischer-Petrosian, Beograd 1970)

White to move

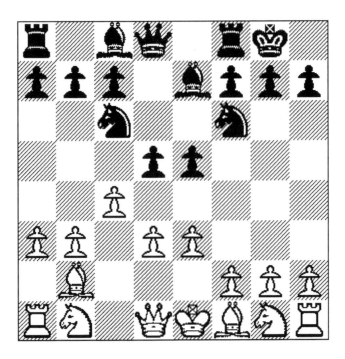

7. cd5!, no doubt this is the best move. White trades semi-central c for opponent central d pawn, which constitutes quite a substantial asset, and, due to its very flexible, although unadvanced, pawn structure, it is much better. Stockfish does not think so, however, preferring black. Frequently, top engines are more of a burden in the opening than an aid. In case white does not capture on d5, black will continue with d5-d4, gaining central space, with evident and real edge this time. 7. d4 fails to 7...ed4 8. ed4 Ne4! 9. Nf3 Bh4 10. g3 Bf6, and the d4 pawn is an excellent target for the black pieces.
(Fischer-Tukmakov, Buenos Aires 1970)

Black to move

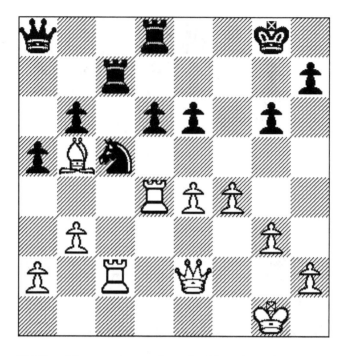

27...e5! The d6 pawn is weak and white should do something about it. e5 simultaneously improves the own knight and makes the opponent bishop worse, with fully equal game(Fischer later even won).

(Damjanovic-Fischer, Buenos Aires 1970)

Black to move

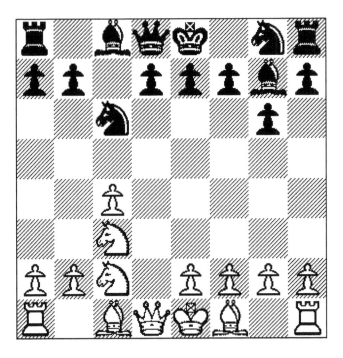

6...Bc3!, the two doubled isolated pawns on the c file will certainly be weaker than the bishop pair in this position of a relatively closed type. Black can later place a knight on c5, safely blocking them, and later attack them, gradually increasing its positional advantages. Alternative moves will make the game more or less equal.

(Quinteros-Fischer, Buenos Aires 1970)

209.

White to move

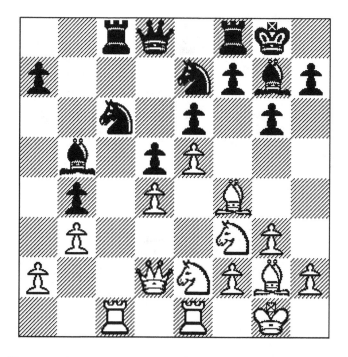

18. g4!, preparing a pawn storm, freeing the g3 square for the e2 knight and taking away the f5 square from the black knight. You really don't need any further considerations to realise this move is the best.

(Fischer-Panno, Buenos Aires 1970)

Black to move

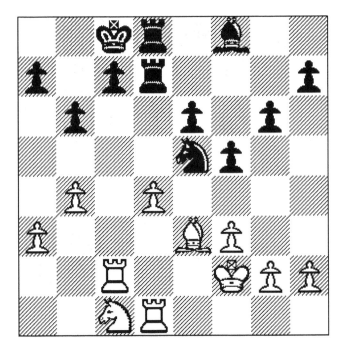

29...b5!, creating an outpost for the black knight on c4 is certainly the best move. 30. de5 capture is impossible because of Rd1.

(Agdamus-Fischer, Buenos Aires 1970)

White to move

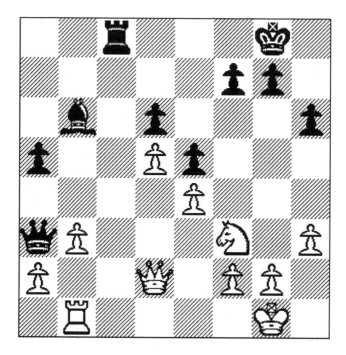

29. Rb2!, an unusual move, with the strategic aim of challenging the black rook on the open c file. After 29...Qc5 30. Ne1(protecting the c2 square to again threaten Rc2) Qc1 31. Qc1 Rc1 32. Kf1 white is much better and still has Rc2 in mind.
(Fischer-Rossetto, Buenos Aires 1970)

White to move

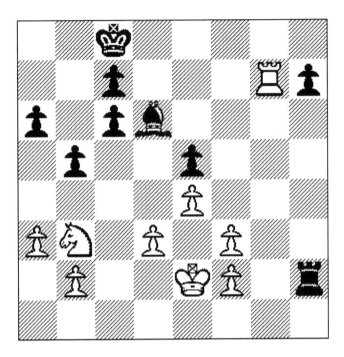

23. f4!, after this temporary sacrifice the white pawn center starts moving, 23...ef4 24. d4 and e5. The f4 pawn is weak and should fall, while the much more active white pieces guarantee an easy win. You really don't need to see any further. If black does not take on f4, then white has d3-d4, with similar developments.
(Fischer-Rubinetti, Buenos Aires 1970)

Black to move

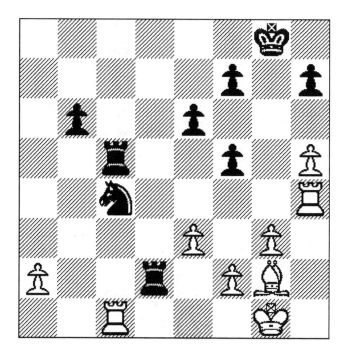

27...Ne5

Black retains a passed pawn both after 28. Rf1 Ra2 and 28. Rc5
Re1 check, followed by dc5. 28. Ra1/b1 Rcc2 is even weaker.
(Smyslov-Fischer, Palma de Mallorca 1970)

214.

Black to move

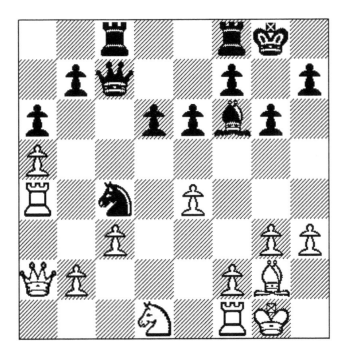

22...Bd8!, attacking the a5 pawn once more and threatening Na5, so that, after the only available move, defending the pawn, b2-b4, the c3 white pawn becomes undefended and weak. A purely positional decision. Sometimes, it is difficult to see such retreats. (Hort-Fischer, Palma de Mallorca 1970)

White to move

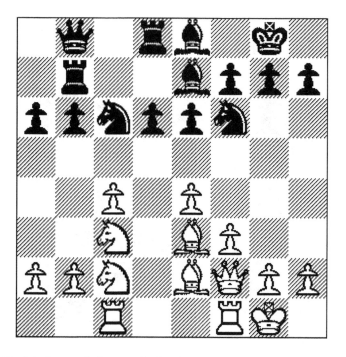

17. a4!, this is a subtle prophylactic move, binding the b5 square. As both b5 and d5 breaks are now impossible for black, white has large advantage(on d6-d5, the a6 pawn will be hanging). A move like 17. g4 is much weaker, due to 17...b5, and black gets nice counterplay. Stockfish will prefer precisely g4 though.
(Fischer-Taimanov, Palma de Mallorca 1970)

Black to move

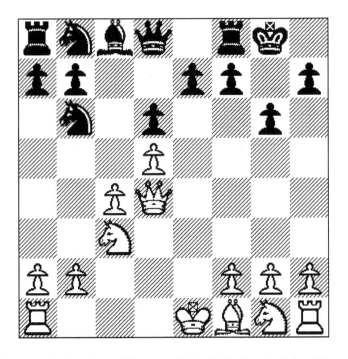

10...e5! Both 11. de6 Be6 and 11. Qd2 f5 give black large
advantage.
(Suttles-Fischer, Palma de Mallorca 1970)

Black to move

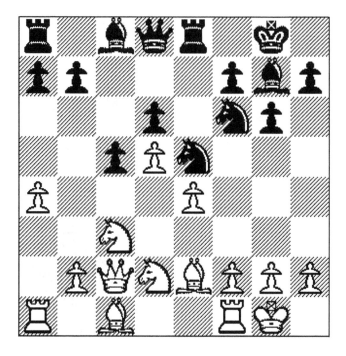

12...g5!, ensuring stability for the knight on e5. Otherwise, f2-f4 threatens all the time, either immediately or after h3 first. A purely positional solution.
(Gligoric-Fischer, Palma de Mallorca 1970)

White to move

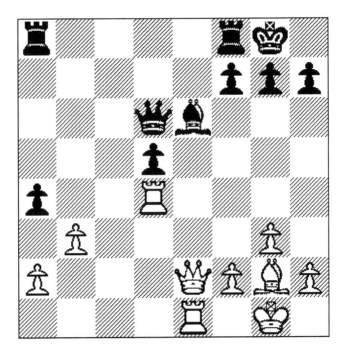

22. b4!, that keeps more material on the board, while at the same time putting the pawn on a square opposite the colour of the own bishop, which makes it stronger. All this promises white good winning chances. 22. ba4 or 22. Ra4 Ra4 23. ba4 are significantly weaker, as material is reduced and the doubled pawns become excellent target for attacks. A similar situation arises, if white allows a ab3 capture. Sometimes, it is important to keep more pawns on the board, in order to convert the advantage.

(Fischer-Nicevski, Rovini-Zagreb 1970)

White to move

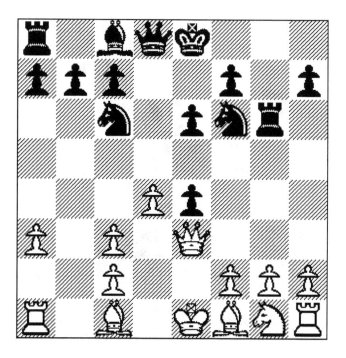

10. Bb2!!, excellent move. The two exclamation marks are for the extreme unusualness of the approach. The king intends to castle long. This is a king side fianchetto on the queen side. One way or another, the king should go somewhere to safety and, as it can not stay in the center or castle short, long castling is the most natural move. At the same time, after castling, the rook will be developed to the central d file with tempo. The move is made even more unusual by the broken-down king shelter, consisting of the c2, c3 and a3 pawns, but the pair of bishops and the close bishop defender on b2 ensure the king a very safe abode. Stockfish completely fails to see that move and, even when it is played, assesses it wrongly.

(Fischer-Uhlmann, Rovini-Zagreb 1970)

White to move

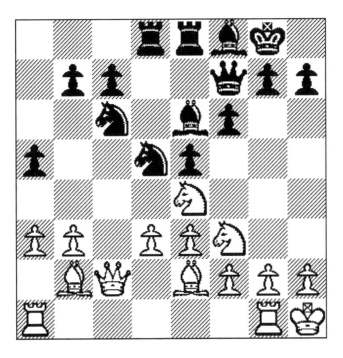

16. g4! Making the e4 knight semi-outposted and threatening Rg1-g3 and Ra1-g1, increasing the attack on the enemy king. Certainly the best move.
(Fischer-Andersson, Siegen 1970)

White to move

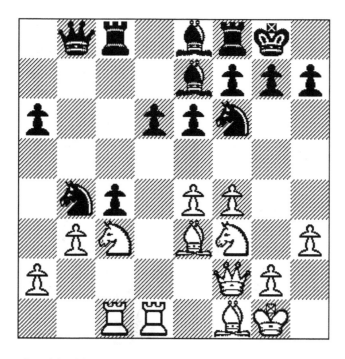

How should white recapture on c4? **23. bc4!**, this is the right move. Although after it the white pawn structure gets severely compromised(both the a2 and c4 pawns are isolated), white keeps the bind upon the central d5 square, which is much more important in this position. The alternative, 23. Bc4, gives black fully equal play after 23...Bc6(24. a3 d5!)

(Fischer-Najdorf, Siegen 1970)

Black to move

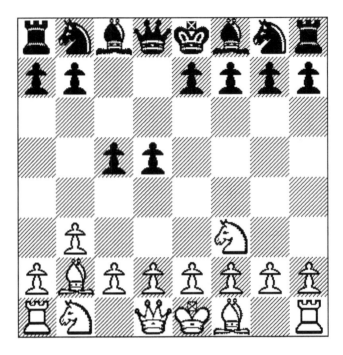

3...f6!, well, believe it or not, this is naturally and obviously the best move. f6 prepares e5, taking valuable central space, and leaves no attack targets to the white bishop on the long diagonal. Why play 3...Nf6 instead, putting the knight on square, where it is attacked by the bishop?
(Petrosian-Fischer, Buenos Aires 1971)

White to move

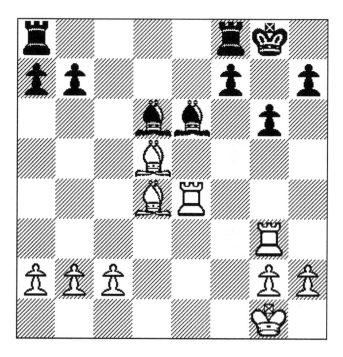

21. Re6! After 21...Bg3(21...fe6?? 22. Be6 Rf7 23. Rf3 Raf8 24. Ba7 is hopeless) 22. Re7 Bd6 23. Rb7 white enjoys some advantage due to the pair of connected passer and potential passer on the c and b files.

(Fischer-Larsen, Denver 1971)

Black to move

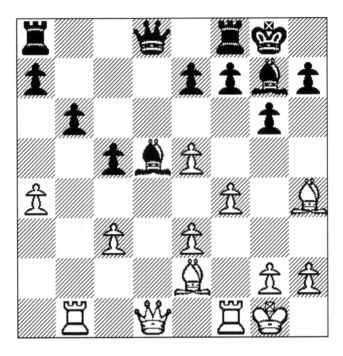

17...f6!, the first thing black should do is increase the mobility of
its dark-square bishop, of course.
(Taimanov-Fischer, Vancouver 1971)

White to move

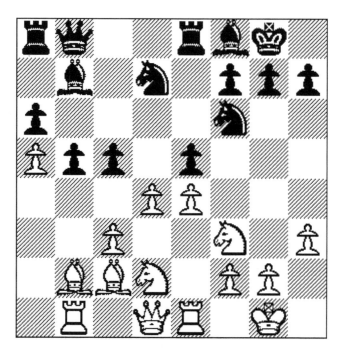

What should white do with the center? **19. de5!**, open it. After
19...Ne5 20. Ne5 Qe5 21. c4 white gets quite some edge. The
alternative, 19. d5, only suits black, leaving it better, as after
19...c4! the black pieces get quite active, the white bishop on b2
somewhat hemmed-in, while after Bd6 is played, the white
central passer on d5 is perfectly blocked. Please note, that after
19. d5 19...Bd6 is a mistake, because of 20.c4!
(Fischer-Spassky, Reykjavik 1972)